8/6/92

Harold,

   To your continued
investment success and
success in all that
you pursue.

                    Terry

Diversified Mutual Fund Investment Strategies

How To Build a High-Return, Low-Risk Portfolio of Mutual Funds

Diversified Mutual Fund Investment Strategies

How To Build a High-Return, Low-Risk Portfolio of Mutual Funds

BY

Terry G. Maxwell

CAPITAL PUBLISHING COMPANY
New York, New York

This publication is designed to provide accurate and
authoritative information in regard to the subject matter
covered. It is sold with the understanding that the
publisher is not engaged in rendering legal, accounting, or
other professional service. If legal advice or other expert
assistance is required, the services of a competent
professional person should be sought.

From a Declaration of Principles jointly adopted by a
Committee of the American Bar Association and
Committee of Publishers.

ISBN 0-9630625-0-6

Library of Congress Catalog Card No. 91-075315

Printed in the United States of America

To my parents, whose love for each other and their family has been an inspiration to us all.

ACKNOWLEDGMENTS

I would like to thank Janiece, my wife and best friend for over ten years, whose support and sacrifices have meant so very much. Without her this book would have not been written.

I would like to acknowledge the immense help and assistance of Ilene Stankiewicz, whose tireless efforts were invaluable in the preparation of this book.

Terry G. Maxwell

Contents

Introduction

I know what you're thinking. Another book on mutual fund investing. While it's true that many books have been written about investing in mutual funds, few of them offer a disciplined investment methodology you can follow to obtain consistently profitable results. Other books may explain what mutual funds are and how they work. They may list the funds available to investors and they may make investment recommendations. But those books often fall short of telling you how to properly structure your portfolio and combine funds to meet your objective. They also don't show you how you can select funds based on their level of risk as well as level of return to truly optimize your portfolio's performance. Those steps, essential for successful investing, are exactly what you will learn by following Diversified Mutual Fund Investing.

Concise and straightforward, DIVERSIFIED MUTUAL FUND INVESTMENT STRATEGIES is a book for novice and experienced investors alike who are looking for a way to increase their rates of return with minimal risk. This book will help you become more fully aware of why your current investments may not be working for you as well as they should be. It will provide you with a logical methodology for structuring your portfolio to achieve your financial objectives. It will show you how you can select the best performing mutual funds based on their relative risk and return. It will also explain how to make certain the funds you choose continue to be the most profitable selections available for your portfolio.

Diversified Mutual Fund Investing, or the process of building a portfolio of mutual funds, presents every investor with an opportunity for profit. Whether your investment objective is income, growth, or some combination of the two, this is a strategy that will work for you. It doesn't matter how much money you have to invest. You don't need to be a financial expert. You won't have to predict the market or interest rate trends.

So how is Diversified Mutual Fund Investing different from just picking a number of different funds? Although investing in mutual funds may be one of the easiest ways to participate in the financial marketplace, it takes more than a variety of funds to assure investment success. It's not even enough to select the best long-term performers. To invest successfully, you need to properly structure your portfolio. Diversified Mutual Fund Investing provides you with a framework for doing just that. You can follow this step-by-step process to first determine your investment objective and then allocate your assets among the mutual fund categories. Recognizing the fact that investors differ in both their objective and risk tolerance, this investment method allows you to easily combine funds in your portfolio and tailor your selections with regard to risk and return.

Diversified Mutual Fund Investing also gives you a sensible means for sorting through all of the funds available. You will see how you can evaluate funds not only by comparing their returns, but by comparing their levels of risk. In this way you can be more confident that your fund selections will be the best performers possible for your particular financial situation.

A portfolio of mutual funds is a simple, yet effective, way to still earn good, consistent returns at a relatively low level of risk. Once you read DIVERSIFIED MUTUAL FUND INVESTMENT STRATEGIES, you will undoubtedly agree that utilizing this systematic, disciplined methodology to properly structure your portfolio, combine funds and select the best relative performers is the safest way to profit in today's market.

Chapter 1

The Categories of Financial Risk

Each time you put your money into stocks, bonds, Certificates of Deposit (CDs) or a savings account, you're taking a risk. Whether or not you've thought about it, where you choose to put your money, in effect, determines the degree of risk you're willing to accept, and the amount of reward you in turn expect. There is such a correlation between investment risk and reward.

Risk can be defined as the possibility of taking a loss. Your risk, in this case, is the possibility of losing money or future income. When you put your money into an account, or you invest in stocks or bonds, you're assuming that your principal will not only be returned, but that you will earn a profit. That doesn't always happen, however.

Different investments involve accepting different types of risk. Those risks are also tied to certain expected levels of reward. If you agree to accept a higher risk, you typically expect a greater reward to compensate you for it. But some investors may be taking a greater risk with their money than they would like, and they may not even be aware of it.

INFLATION RISK

What happens to your money when you purchase CDs? Your money is locked in for a pre-determined length of time earning a fixed rate of interest. At the end of that time period, you will get your principal back, plus interest. Would you consider this to be a safe way to make money?

Consider the following situation:

A 63-year-old man who will be retiring in two years is looking for a way to provide some added income after he retires. He has worked hard all his life to acquire his wealth. His current assets total over $600,000, although much of that sum is tied up in personal assets that cannot be used to produce income, such as his homes and cars. He has approximately $150,000 in CDs, and earning just over $100,000 per year, describes himself as a very conservative investor. He feels his CDs are very safe and he doesn't want to worry about the risks other investments present. Even if his CDs earn only 7 percent, he says he wants to count on his money earning interest and on the return of his principal. In short, he wants to make money, yet he doesn't want to be concerned about taking any losses.

It's easy to understand why this man wants to keep his money secure. He doesn't want to lose any of his earnings at this point in his life. But even though CDs are insured by the federal government, they're hardly risk-free. This soon-to-retire man has been lulled into a false sense of security by ignoring the effects of inflation. Inflation involves the purchasing power of your money, meaning how much it is worth over time when exchanged for goods and services. The Consumer Price Index measures inflation, or the rate of change in the prices of consumer goods. When inflation rises, there is a corresponding increase in the cost of living and the cost of goods and services. What really happens is our dollar loses value and, in turn, purchasing power; it takes more dollars to buy the same amount of goods and services than it did in the past.

Given today's longer life expectancies, this man and his wife may very well live another 20 years or more. During that time the cost of living will undoubtedly increase. Yet even if they spend only the interest from their CDs, they are still risking the possibility that their money will be insufficient to meet their future financial needs.

Figure 1 shows what will happen to the value of the couple's $100,000 over 30 years based on different rates of inflation. Over time, they will lose the value of their capital, exactly what our retiree did not want to have happen. And they may not be aware that they're losing money.

Figure 1

Effects of Inflation on $100,000

Time Period	3%	5%	7%
1 Year	$97,087	$95,238	$93,458
2 Years	$94,260	$90,703	$87,344
3 Years	$91,514	$86,384	$81,630
4 Years	$88,849	$82,270	$76,290
5 Years	$86,261	$78,353	$71,299
6 Years	$83,748	$74,622	$66,634
7 Years	$81,309	$71,068	$62,275
8 Years	$78,941	$67,684	$58,201
9 Years	$76,642	$64,461	$54,393
10 Years	$74,409	$61,391	$50,835
15 Years	$64,186	$48,102	$36,245
20 Years	$55,368	$37,689	$25,842
25 Years	$47,761	$29,530	$18,425
30 Years	$41,199	$23,138	$13,137

If, for example, the annual inflation rate is 5 percent, in just five years the couple's $100,000 will be worth only $78,353. In 10 years they will lose almost $40,000 of the value of their money. And in 25 years their money will be worth less than one-third of the original $100,000.

What happens to the corresponding value of the interest from their CDs if inflation remains at a 5 percent annual rate? Just like their principal, it will lose value. If the CDs are paying 7 percent interest, in the first year they will earn $7,000. In five years that $7,000 in interest will be worth $5,485; in 10 years it will be worth $4,297; and in 25 years the interest will be worth less than one-third of the $7,000. What will happen if inflation moves up to 7 percent or more per year? Their loss of principal value will be accelerated.

Many investors do not realize how detrimental inflation can be over time. Although inflation has averaged 3 percent annually from the end of 1925 through 1987, according to a study by Roger G. Ibbotson and Rex A. Sinquefield, it has been as high as 13.3 percent in one year (1979). When you purchase CDs, you want to get your money back, plus enough interest so you can buy the same things you bought previously with fewer dollars. The same is true for money in your savings account or any other fixed-interest investment. If the rate of return on your investment is not greater than the rate of inflation, you risk losing purchasing power.

Treasury bills (T-bills) are short-term investments that are considered to be relatively risk-free. Over the

last 60 years, however, a T-bill investor would have
had returns only 0.5 percent greater than the inflation
rate, according to the Ibbotson and Sinquefield study.
Historically, T-bills have had rates of return similar to
money markets and short-term CDs. So those CDs
would also have had a return of approximately 0.5 percent above the inflation rate.

Taxes are another very real factor that we all face.
What happens when we consider the effect of taxes on
our money in addition to inflation? If we adjust the 7
percent return on our retiree's CDs for a 28 percent
federal tax rate, in addition to the 5 percent we have
already subtracted for inflation, our investor's $7,000
annual return will shrink even more. Figure 2 shows
the effects.

Figure 2

Effect of Inflation and Taxes On a
Fixed-Interest Return

Time Period	Inflation	Taxes and Inflation
1st Year	$7,000	$5,040
5th Year	$5,485	$3,949
10th Year	$4,297	$3,094
25th Year	$2,067	$1,488

Inflation assumption 5%, Tax rate assumption 28%

The first year's return on the couple's $100,000 again will come to $7,000. If we factor in a 28 percent tax rate, the return drops to $5,040. After five years, their $7,000 return will be worth $5,485 if we account for inflation; it drops to $3,949 after taxes. Look what happens after 25 years: Inflation eats up their $7,000 return by more than two-thirds, and after taxes less than one-quarter of their original return remains.

Inflation is an even greater threat to long-term investments since it's more difficult to predict what inflation rates will be three, five, or more years from now. No one knows what it will cost to buy a bag of groceries in 10 years. If you're locked into an investment paying a rate of interest lower than the inflation rate, you lose, especially once you add in the effect of taxes.

As an investor, you need to be concerned about how inflation will affect your returns. You can see that while inflation is the risk that gets the least attention, it is a continuous threat to your long-term purchasing power and your financial security. Your investment plans should include compensating for the effects of inflation. You can ignore inflation, but inflation won't ignore your money.

MARKET RISK

Through the years, stocks have been the most effective investments for overcoming inflation by providing investors with dividends and/or capital appreciation. According to Ibbotson and Sinquefield's publication *Stocks, Bonds, Bills and Inflation*, stocks have historically outperformed all other investment vehicles.

Figure 3

Wealth Indexes of Investments
in U.S. Capital Markets (1926-1987)
(Year End 1925 = 1.00)

Figure 3 illustrates how well stocks have performed in comparison to other investments. The figure, based on Ibbotson and Sinquefield's data, covers the 62-year period from year-end 1925 to 1987. It includes all types of events that affected the market during that time.

As the figure shows, if you had invested $1.00 in small company stocks at the end of 1925 and reinvested all of your dividends, the return on your dollar would have been $1,202.97 at the end of 1987. By comparison, if you had invested $1.00 in long-term government bonds, you would have had $13.35 in 1987. And $1.00 invested in U.S. Treasury bills would have returned $8.37. What a difference! Investors who simply held their positions in stocks over the years would have fared better than those who invested in any type of bonds. Inflation alone ran 3 percent per year on average over this time period, inflating $1.00 worth of goods and services up to $6.44 in 1987. Thus, $1.00 invested in T-bills in 1925 would have grown to only $1.36 by 1987, considering inflation.

But most of us invest amounts much greater than $1.00 and the performance of our investments over time becomes even more crucial. Let's take a look at how an investor would have fared with a $10,000 investment. Figure 4 compares the 1987 values of $10,000 invested in different investment vehicles in 1925, before and after adjusting for a 3 percent rate of inflation. Again, the top performers would have been small company stocks, with a compound annual return of 12.1 percent before accounting for inflation. If you had invested in common stocks, you would have averaged an annual gain of 9.9 percent. Treasury bills returned just 3.5 percent.

Figure 4

1987 Value of $10,000 Invested at Year-End 1925
(all dividends reinvested)

Type of Investment	Total Returns	Annual Return	Inflation Adjusted	Real Return
Small Company Stocks	$12,029,700	12.1%	$2,213,780	9.1%
Common Stocks	$ 3,479,600	9.9%	$ 626,063	6.9%
Long-term Gov't. Bonds	$ 133,500	4.3%	$ 22,273	1.3%
Treasury Bills	$ 83,700	3.5%	$ 13,624	0.5%

* Inflation adjusted at 3%

Now, look what happens to returns when we account for inflation. Your $10,000 invested in common stocks would have lost $2,853,537 in value to inflation by 1987; your real return would have been 6.9 percent. Treasury bills are still on the bottom, returning only 0.5 percent after inflation. Small company stocks remain at the top, returning $221.37 for every dollar you invested in 1925 and leaving you with over $2 million even after your return is inflation-adjusted.

It's quite obvious that for longer holding periods, stocks offer you the chance to make tremendous gains on your investment dollars. Short-term, however, stocks can be volatile investments; the market can fluctuate widely and unpredictably, influencing the price of your shares, sometimes arbitrarily. Investors in the stock market must be willing to accept this market risk, or the chance that the overall stock market will rise and fall and affect their investment.

Market risk can be measured in various ways, one of which is "beta." Beta is a numerical measure of short-term price volatility relative to the volatility of the stock market as a whole. Beta measures are derived from the Standard & Poor's Composite Index of stocks from 500 of the largest publicly held companies (S&P 500). The S&P 500 has a beta value of 1.00, which is considered average volatility; stocks with a beta value of 1.00 cycle up and down with the same volatility as the S&P 500. Stocks that are more volatile than the market have beta values higher than 1.00 and fluctuate more than the S&P 500. Stocks that are less volatile than the market have beta values of less than 1.00 and fluctuate less than the S&P 500.

Another measure of market risk is "return volatility," which is nothing more than the range of returns, or the extent to which actual returns vary from the average. As with beta, the wider the range of returns, the greater the volatility, and the more likely it is that your return will deviate from the average return. This deviation can be either positive or negative.

Figure 5 compares the range of total compound annual returns for different investment vehicles from 1925 through 1987. Small company stocks produced the highest average annual returns over the 62-year period, but they also fluctuated over the widest range – from a high of 142.9 percent in 1933, to a low of minus 58 percent in 1937. If you had put your money in T-bills, you would have had the lowest average return, but your return would have fluctuated the least – from a high of 14.7 percent to a low of zero.

Figure 5

Range of Total Annual Returns
1925-1987

Type of Investment	High	Average	Low
Small Company Stocks	142.9%	12.1%	-58.0%
Common Stocks	54.0%	9.9%	-43.3%
Long-term Government Bonds	40.4%	4.9%	- 9.2%
Treasury Bills	14.7%	3.5%	0%

Bonds are affected by their own type of market risk in the form of interest rate fluctuations. Interest rates were once relatively stable and bonds were considered to have much less risk than stocks. In some years, however, the bond market has actually been more volatile than the stock market, especially with respect to long-term bonds.

All bonds move up or down in value in relation to daily changes in interest rates. Even though you receive a fixed rate of interest, the principal value of your bonds will continue to fluctuate. Every percentage point that interest rates fluctuate will have an inverse effect on the value of your bonds. The value of your bonds will decrease when interest rates rise; the value will increase when interest rates fall. What happens is that when interest rates rise, newer bonds are issued at higher rates, making your lower-interest bonds less attractive to investors and thus less valuable. But if interest rates drop, your bonds become more valuable and more attractive to investors because they will pay a higher rate of interest than the new bonds being issued. You will not actually realize a gain or a loss on your principal until you cash in your bonds.

The Benham Capital Management chart in Figure 6 shows how even a 1 percent change in interest rates will affect a $10,000 bond investment. Although U.S. Treasury securities return 100 percent of their face value if held to maturity, the figures in the chart reflect possible capital appreciation or loss if the securities are sold before maturity.

Figure 6

Changes in the Market Value of a $10,000 Investment

Type of Bond	A 1% increase in interest rates decreases bond values by:	A 1% decrease in interest rates increases bond values by:
Treasury Notes (5-year maturity)	$ 383	$ 401
Treasury Notes (10-year maturity)	$ 617	$ 672
Treasury Bonds (30-year maturity)	$ 940	$1,123
Zero-coupon Bonds (30-year maturity)	$1,989	$2,665

As you can see in Figure 6, a 1 percent rise in interest rates will decrease the value of a five-year Treasury note by $383; if interest rates fall by 1 percent, the value will increase by $401. By comparison, 10-year Treasury notes have greater volatility; each 1 percent fluctuation in interest rates will cause 10-year Treasury notes to fluctuate in value by over $600. As bond maturities increase, so does the market risk. If you increase bond maturities to 30 years, volatility also increases. Although there is a greater potential for a 30-year bond to increase in value, there is also a greater risk that it will lose value. Zero coupon bonds – those that accrue interest for a lump sum payment at maturity – would have the greatest risk of losing value.

Default Risk

When compared to government bonds, corporate bonds have provided investors with higher returns. Like other bonds, corporate bonds are subject to market risk. But they have an added risk – the risk of default. When you invest in a bond, you are, in effect lending money in exchange for timely payments of interest and principal. With corporate bonds, there is the chance that the company will be unable to make its scheduled interest payments to bondholders and will default.

Bonds vary in quality and are rated according to the issuing company's credit stability. Standard & Poor's and Moody's are two companies that rate bonds. Bond quality ratings, as shown in Figure 7, basically tell an investor how reliable the company is in paying borrowers. The rating is also an indication of corporate credit risk.

Figure 7

Bond Ratings

Standard & Poor's	Moody's	Quality
AAA	Aaa	Prime
AA	Aa	Excellent
A	A-1, A	Upper Medium
BBB	Baa-1, Baa	Lower Medium
BB	Ba	Speculative
B, CCC, CC	B, Caa	Very Speculative
Ca, C	D	Default

Creditworthy companies have the best records of payment. They issue bonds that have higher quality ratings and are considered to have less risk of default. Since return is tied to the amount of risk taken, these high-grade bonds offer a lower rate of interest. Conversely, a bond with a lower-quality rating is considered to have a higher risk of default and will pay a higher rate of interest. Although there is a possibility that companies offering high-grade securities will default, companies offering low-quality bonds are most subject to this risk.

The lowest-rated bonds, grade B or lower, are considered to be below investment grade and are better known as "junk" bonds. Junk bonds are issued by companies that have less credit-worthiness. It would stand to reason that junk bonds would have the highest risk of default. But junk bonds pay a higher interest rate to compensate investors for assuming this risk.

THE RISK-RETURN TRADEOFF

Every investor would like to earn high returns on investments without assuming the associated high risk. When it comes to investing, however, there is a risk-return tradeoff. Although the link between risk and return is not necessarily direct and predictable, relatively speaking the higher the reward you seek, the more risk you must accept. Investments that are considered risky tend to compensate investors with the potential for higher returns, as well they should. If you reduce your downside risk, you also reduce your chances for higher profits.

Investors who put their money in T-bills and CDs may have "safety" of principal, but they have been rewarded with what have historically been the lowest returns. This low return is related to the lower level of risk. Yet even these lower returns will not keep inflation from eroding your purchasing power. Inflation will prey upon your principal as well as your return.

Bond investors have historically received a better rate of return than T-bill and CD investors. Still, both government and corporate bonds are subject to market risk. We have seen a dramatic increase in bond market volatility in reaction to fluctuating interest rates. Bonds have less market risk on a short-term basis. Longer-term bonds may provide higher returns, but they are subject to greater market risk. Corporate bonds add the risk of default.

No matter how you look at it, stocks have provided investors with the highest returns. Although stocks have had the best long-term record of protecting investor dollars against inflation, this high rate of return has not been without risk. Stock investors can be amply rewarded, but they must be willing to assume market risk. Stock investors must be prepared, in some years, to make little money, or lose a portion of their investment dollars.

As an investor, you need to look at the risk as well as the reward. Every investment involves risk and you will always face at least one type – inflation risk, market risk, default risk – or some combination of all three. An understanding of the risks over various time periods may be just as important as understanding the potential returns; you will be in a better position to determine whether the risks are worth accepting. If you are aware of the risks and know how to deal with them you are also more likely to realize greater profits than if you disregard the risks. Investment risks will always be present whether you acknowledge them or not.

Chapter 2

Investing in Mutual Funds

If you have $100,000 that you want to invest with an opportunity for reasonable profits and relative safety, where do you begin? You could try picking your own stocks and bonds if you were willing to commit a number of hours each day to the time-consuming task of poring over research materials and financial data bases. You could turn to a broker, and assume the difficulties associated with the brokerage industry, principally the conflict of interest that arises between recommending suitable investments and selling products that will earn the highest commissions. You could hire your own money manager to select stocks and bonds for your portfolio as many larger institutions do; however, you often need a minimum account of $1 million to attract one of the best. Yet it would be ideal to have a full-time, highly experienced professional taking care of your hard-earned money and carefully selecting an array of securities for your portfolio to meet your investment objective.

More small and large investors alike are discovering that they can have the benefits of professional money management, reviewable records of performance, and diversification, cost-effectively, by investing in mutual funds. There are so many mutual funds available that all investors should be able to find funds which are suitable for their investment needs. Mutual funds also typically require low minimum investments because they combine the money of many investors who have a similar investment objective.

THE GROWTH OF FUNDS

Mutual funds have been in existence for over 100 years in one form or another. The fund idea originated with British and Scottish investment trusts in the 1860s. Robert Fleming, a Scottish immigrant, is credited with bringing the fund concept to America in the late 1800s. Fleming came to America to make his fortune, but found he and his friends couldn't cash in on the country's great investment wealth individually. They decided to pool their capital and invest only in high-grade bonds in stable industries. That was the start of the Scottish-American Investment Trust, formed in 1873. It was diversified, carefully managed, efficiently run, and the investors were able to profit.

American brokers soon seized upon the fund idea and began to create investment pools of their own. These grew into what are now known as "closed-end" mutual funds. Shares of closed-end mutual funds trade similarly to stock and are bought and sold on an exchange. A fixed number of shares are issued and the buy and sell price is determined by supply and demand. Shares may be bought at a discount, for less than their actual value. Shares may also be bought at a premium, or for more than their actual value, if the demand is high enough. Although buyers always hope to sell their shares for a higher price than they paid for them, shares of closed-end funds also may have to be sold at a discount. Regular commissions are charged on closed-end fund shares regardless of whether shares are bought or sold at a premium or discount.

More investors are familiar with open-end funds, on which this book will concentrate. Open-end funds were first formed in 1924 by the Massachusetts Investment Trust and State Street Investment Corporation. Unlike companies that issue stock, open-end funds continuously issue new shares to anyone who wishes to invest and the number of existing shares is constantly changing. Fund shares are purchased and redeemed at the current price per share, otherwise known as the "net asset value." The net asset value is determined by tallying the total value of the fund's portfolio at the end of the business day, subtracting the day's expenses, and dividing by the number of existing shares.

Open-end funds may be purchased directly from the investment company by mail or through a broker, brokerage firm or other financial institution. Open-end funds are listed under "mutual funds" in most daily newspapers.

Over the years, the growth of funds, in both the number available to investors and the dollar amount invested, has increased dramatically, as Figure 8 illustrates. According to information from The Investment Company Institute in Washington, D.C., the number of funds available to investors did not change very much from 1940 to 1960. But over the next 10 years, the number of mutual funds jumped from 161 to 361 as investors began to accept the fund concept as a legitimate investment vehicle. Still, it wasn't until the 1970s that mutual funds really became popular. It was also at that time that money market funds and short-term municipal bond funds were added to the list of alternatives available to the public.

Figure 8

Number of Mutual Funds Available to Investors

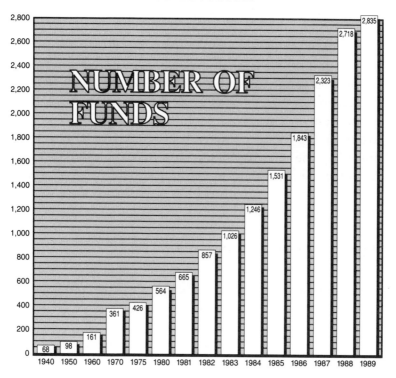

The tremendous growth in both the number of funds available and the total invested assets has continued. Between 1980 and 1985, nearly 1,000 additional funds were started. Millions of individuals who never owned a stock or bond bought shares of mutual funds in the

1980s. In 1984, funds were selling at a record $45 billion annually. In 1986, investors poured a whopping $215 billion into funds. Total assets invested in mutual funds rose from $448 million in 1940 to a phenomenal $810 billion in 1988.

This immense popularity of mutual funds has by no means been limited to small, individual investors, either. By the end of 1984, institutional investors represented 38 percent of all mutual fund assets, not including IRA or Keogh accounts. Looking at it dollarwise, in 1970 institutions had just over $6 billion invested in funds, while in 1984 their holdings had climbed to $140 billion. By the end of 1988, institutional investors held $261.9 billion worth of mutual funds.

How Funds Operate

Following the 1929 market crash, Congress provided a framework for mutual fund operations known as the Investment Company Act of 1940, that made mutual fund investment companies highly regulated. The Investment Company Act prevents any form of self-dealing or conflicts of interest. In addition, many states have their own fund regulations.

Among other requirements, a fund must register with the Securities and Exchange Commission (SEC) before making its shares available to investors. A fund must have a specific operating structure and philosophy, provide potential investors with a prospectus, and provide both shareholders and the SEC with regular, detailed accounting and performance reports.

The prospectus is required by law to disclose everything pertinent about the fund and fund activities. It contains information which includes the fund's investment objectives and strategies, policies, officers and directors, services, methods of purchasing and redeeming shares, expenses and fees, reinvestment alternatives, financial statements and investment restrictions. The prospectus will also provide you with information on a fund's historical performance and current holdings. You can obtain this document from the fund by either calling or writing. Many funds have toll-free numbers that can be found in various financial publications.

Some funds have a separate "Form B" or "Statement of Additional Information" that contains information on fees and portfolio holdings which may not appear in the prospectus. It also provides per share financial information for the 10 most recent fiscal years, if the fund has been in existence that long. Data relating to investment income, operating expenses, dividends, gains or losses on securities, and net asset values are included. Form B is not usually presented to prospective shareholders unless requested.

Mutual funds are corporations chartered by states to conduct business as investment companies. As such, each fund must have an investment advisor/manager, an independent board of directors, an independent transfer agent and a custodian. The investment company's sole business and purpose is to pool the money of investors into a single portfolio of securities. At least 75 percent of a fund's assets must be invested at all times, with not more than 5 percent in any one security and not more than 10 percent in any one corporation if that 10 percent has voting privileges.

Although fund directors take care of business, the fund is owned by the shareholders. It is the shareholders who elect board members and approve operating policies or any changes in fund objectives. The fund's board hires a "manager" to act as an investment advisor for the fund. The manager may be an individual or a firm that assigns a team of researchers and analysts under a senior manager to control the fund. The fund manager may also manage other mutual or pension funds.

By law, the assets of a mutual fund must be held in trust by a third party, such as a custodian bank or trust company; you send your money directly to the financial institution. The transfer agent, also a bank or trust company, is responsible for issuing or transferring fund shares and maintaining shareholder records. Often a single bank serves as both custodian and transfer agent.

As a mutual fund shareholder, you have a direct claim on your assets at all times. You also have a right to vote on any change in the fund's status. Except in extreme cases, a fund cannot suspend redemptions and tie up your account. For example, your fund redemption can be held up only if the New York Stock Exchange closes for reasons other than a weekend or holiday, or if the SEC declares a general emergency and suspends all trading. A mutual fund cannot go bankrupt in the same way other companies might. In theory, if fund directors determine it is no longer profitable or sensible to remain in operation, a fund can ask its shareholders for permission to terminate business. The most likely way for a fund to cease operating, however, is by merging into a larger fund. Shareholders of the first fund will automatically become investors in the second fund.

Funds are required to return a minimum of over 90 percent of their profits to investors. Profits are paid out in two ways: dividends from the fund's underlying stocks and bonds; and capital gains, which are the net gains on the sale of portfolio holdings.

All funds have expenses that are paid out of the fund's income and all investors pay a portion of those expenses. Fund expenses consist of annual management or advisory fees and administrative overhead that includes legal services, auditing and printing. Some funds charge a nominal annual paperwork fee of somewhere between $10 and $30.

Some funds also charge annual 12b-1 fees. These fees were first authorized in 1980 and allow mutual funds to use a certain portion of fund assets to pay for marketing and distribution expenses. Thus, 12b-1 fees pay for sales literature and advertising as well as commissions to brokers. In the past, mutual funds had to pay these expenses from their own share of the profits and recoup the costs from sales fees if possible. Now 12b-1 charges are deducted from the total return numbers you see for the fund.

Load funds are mutual funds that charge a sales commission similar to the commission on a stock or bond trade, but larger. Load funds are typically sold by brokers, but also through financial planners, insurance agents and others. A "load" is a one-time percentage of the money you invest that is used to pay commissions. Fund loads may be as high as 8.5 percent on your investments under $10,000. If you invest larger amounts of money, you will pay a lower percentage load. Or, if you buy shares of several funds in the same fund family at once, they will be treated as a single purchase and you will pay a reduced load. There are also low-load funds that charge a load of 3 percent or 4 percent.

Funds may have a front-end or back-end load. With a front-end load, a percentage is taken out before your money is invested in the fund. Front-end loads are reflected in a fund's higher per share "buy" price. Back-end loads, or deferred sales charges, are paid when you sell your fund shares. Funds with deferred sales charges may require that you pay the full charge upon withdrawal, but more often they have declining withdrawal charges. This deferred charge generally begins at 5 percent or 6 percent and declines by 1 percent for each year you hold your shares until it disappears.

No-load funds do not charge any up-front fees or commissions when you buy shares; all of your money is invested in the fund. No-load fund shares are usually offered directly to investors by the fund, so there are no salespeople to compensate. Sometimes investors will be misled into thinking that a fund with a deferred sales charge is a no-load, which it is not. True no-loads do not charge deferred sales fees. Although no-load funds are permitted to charge 12b-1 fees, it is more typical for expenses of that type to be paid out of fund earnings.

Some funds charge only a very small sales fee if you should decide to sell your shares within a relatively short period of time, say within 90 days of investing. This is not a load, but a fee used by the fund to recoup costs that would have been covered by returns on your investment had you held the shares for a longer time. It may also be used to discourage investors from frequently selling shares.

Besides reading a fund's prospectus, you can determine which fees a fund charges by looking through the mutual fund listings in many daily newspapers. Figure 9 interprets some of the symbols found in a newspaper's mutual fund listings.

Figure 9

Fund Fees

Symbol	Meaning
NL	In the fund's "buy" column, this indicates a no-load fund.
p	The fund charges a distribution and marketing (12b-1) fee.
r	The fund has a redemption charge. The charge may begin at a certain point and gradually diminish until it disappears.
t or **p** and **r**	Sometimes "t" is substituted for "p" and "r" when a fund charges both a 12b-1 and redemption fee.

WHY INVEST IN MUTUAL FUNDS

We've seen how the volatility of the market, and to some extent the abundance of choices, has changed the investment environment. It's no longer as simple as it once was to select stocks and bonds for your portfolio. You have to take the time to make certain you select sound issues with a demonstrated potential for profit. You have to be broadly diversified to sufficiently reduce your risk. And you have to constantly watch your portfolio and the market.

There are many reasons to invest in mutual funds, but the three major benefits are professional management, reviewable records of performance and diversification.

PROFESSIONAL MANAGEMENT

Managing money requires expertise and discipline. It also requires full-time attention. Studies have shown that many individual investors underperform the market or lose money because they just don't have the time to devote to proper investment analysis. Larger institutions can, of course, afford to hire their own team of specialists – analysts, money managers and senior investment officers – to study how economic trends might affect the market and their investments. As an individual investor, you can get the same professional money management as these large institutions, even more efficiently, by investing in mutual funds.

Professional money management is an important benefit available to all mutual fund investors. When you buy shares in a mutual fund you know your dollars will automatically hire a full-time investment professional and a management team whose job it is to select securities in a way most of us don't have the time or resources to do adequately.

Unlike brokers, fund managers are not involved in marketing; all of their time is devoted to managing the fund. In addition, they do not have to provide any client services or answer client questions. They do not have to explain why they chose a particular investment for the fund. They can make investment decisions and implement their strategy based on their own statistical analysis and professional judgment. The final determinant of a fund manager's success is the fund's returns, not whether every investor is satisfied with the manner in which the fund's assets have been invested.

Once you select a fund that will meet your objective, you need not be overly concerned about the ups and downs of every market cycle. It is the fund manager's job to keep track of companies and the economy, and buy and sell individual securities for the fund. Committed to fund performance, managers are in a position to take advantage of opportunities when they occur and to realize profits. When the market rises, you can benefit from those advances through a fund manager's buys. And when the market falls, there will be less downside risk than if you were holding individual issues.

How do you know the best money managers aren't working only for private individual or institutional accounts? Investment companies, like any other business, want to attract investors and generate favorable returns. Thus, some of the top managers in the country are hired to manage mutual funds. Their expertise will serve to draw investor dollars into the fund and earn a profit for the investment company as well as for investors.

Clearly Stated Investment Objectives and Fund Strategy

Mutual funds are required to clearly state their objectives in the fund prospectus. And according to SEC regulations, mutual fund managers must adhere to the fund's objectives and by-laws. If, for example, your objective is income and you select a fund that has an income objective, the fund manager must invest in income-producing securities and not in speculative stock issues.

On what basis will fund investments be made? How will individual stocks and bonds be selected for the fund's portfolio? The fund's prospectus must answer these questions. The prospectus must state the fund's investment strategy, which is to say it must tell you how the investment objective will be pursued.

In addition, potential investors can examine the fund's portfolio to see exactly where fund dollars are being invested. The portfolio's composition is another indication of how a fund's objective is being followed. Fund portfolio information can be found in the fund's prospectus or the Statement of Additional Information.

REVIEWABLE RECORDS OF PERFORMANCE

If you are presented with a broker's or a private investment manager's statement of past performance, you have no way of knowing whether the statement covers all accounts, or specially selected accounts representing the top performing portfolios.

While there are no rules governing how private investment managers or brokers report results, the same is not true of mutual funds. Mutual funds must keep daily performance records, as well as filing annual reports with the Securities and Exchange Commission. In addition, a mutual fund's performance data are readily accessible to investors.

Audited Results

The Investment Company Act of 1940 requires that all mutual funds file an audited record of the returns the fund has obtained for the year. Whether the fund's results are exceptional or average, they are scrutinized and then recorded.

Documented Long-Term Performance

Investors can easily review a fund's performance records for as many years as the fund has been in existence. Historical data on the fund's performance can be obtained from sources that include the library, the fund itself, or statistical services. Some of the services which compile these data for investors include Lipper Analytical Services, Weisenberger Investment Services and CDA Investment Technologies. Such records make it simpler for you to examine past performance, compare funds over a number of years and make decisions.

It's highly unlikely a private investment manager would be as open regarding personal performance.

A Daily Record of Performance

You may receive quarterly statements from some of your investments and your bank may provide you with monthly statements, but a mutual fund is required to calculate its returns every business day. A mutual fund, once again, must be prepared to redeem shares at their net asset value at the close of each business day. This requirement also creates a daily public record of a fund's (and fund manager's) performance. The net asset value of fund shares can be found in the financial section of many newspapers. These statistics then form the basis of long-term performance records.

DIVERSIFICATION

Every investor has heard the phrase "don't put all your eggs in one basket." That's certainly still true. Today many investors are making diversification a top priority, as well they should. Diversifying your portfolio reduces your risk and improves your chances for profit.

Diversification is one area in which mutual funds excel. Investing in a mutual fund offers all investors diversification on three different levels.

Asset Diversification

Mutual funds allow you to diversify your investment among different asset categories. You can select funds that invest in stocks, bonds or money markets. These categories of funds perform differently from each other and each category is best suited for meeting a specific investment objective. An income investor can select from bond funds, growth investors can select from stock funds and money market funds can be used for liquidity needs.

Security Diversification

If you own shares in only a few companies and any one of them takes a downturn, your entire portfolio could be severely affected. But a single mutual fund may be diversified among many companies and every share represents an investment that may be divided up among dozens of different stocks and bonds or cash equivalents. As an investor, you benefit directly from such diversification. Mutual funds allow you to participate in a wider portion of the market than you likely could on your own, thus spreading your risk over many companies and industries. A diverse portfolio of investments protects you in the event that any one holding in the portfolio loses value. Unlike a portfolio with limited diversification, even if several issues in the fund decline, overall the fund can still profit.

Management and Style Diversification

The wide selection of mutual funds also provides investors with choices of fund management. There are different fund management styles as well as different fund managers. Fund managers will differ in how they invest fund assets for growth, income or a combination of growth and income. There are fund managers who will invest in large companies and small companies. There are fund managers who will invest in specialized areas of the market. A fund manager can, therefore, have a strong influence on a fund's performance while adhering to the fund's stated investment objective and strategy.

As a mutual fund investor, you are free to select a manager and management style you are comfortable with. If you hire a professional money manager and aren't satisfied with the results, your situation can be difficult to change. It can take time to find another manager, liquidate your portfolio and reinvest your money elsewhere. If you are not satisfied with a mutual fund manager's performance, there are many more fund managers you can choose from, and you can reinvest in another fund rather easily.

ADDITIONAL BENEFITS

Besides the three major advantages of professional management, reviewable records of performance and diversification, mutual funds provide investors with several other important benefits. Mutual funds are cost-effective. Funds incur lower transaction costs because they have tremendous buying power. They purchase such large quantities of securities that they qualify for commission discounts.

Investors will find that mutual funds offer them flexibility. With most funds, you can receive your fund distributions or you can have them automatically reinvested, which is something not easily done with individual stocks or bonds. Although dividends and capital gains distributions are taxable even if they are reinvested, reinvesting increases your holdings and the compounding on your investment. Moreover, you can add investment dollars to your mutual fund account at a later date and you can purchase fractional fund shares.

You often have similar options when it comes to making fund withdrawals. You can choose to make partial withdrawals instead of having to sell off all of your holdings. Some mutual funds offer additional conveniences, including check writing or telephone exchange privileges. Through telephone exchanges you can quickly and easily switch investment dollars between funds in the same "family" instead of opening a new account. You can, for example, switch between income and growth funds within a fund family. Most of the time you can switch between funds at no cost, or at a very nominal $5 or $10 charge.

If you need your money, or if you wish to get out of a fund for any reason, you can liquidate your shares with relative ease. All open-end mutual funds must honor buy and sell orders on the day they are received, provided they are received before the fund's daily cut-off time. Your shares will be redeemed at the fund's net asset value at the close of the day's business. You can move money in and out of a mutual fund by mail at almost any time and in almost any amount. Sometimes redeeming fund shares takes nothing more than a phone call, although most funds still require a letter with a signature guaranteed by a national bank. In the case of a letter, the fund must process your request on the day your letter is received and mail your redemption check within seven days.

Chapter 3

Factors in
Fund Selection

Three years ago an investor put his money into a fund listed as one of the year's top 10 performers. He, of course, expected superior returns. Given the fund's ranking, that would seem a reasonable assumption. A year later, however, the fund's returns plummeted; it was one of the year's worst performers. Becoming disillusioned with the fund, the investor sold out at a low point and took a loss.

This is one example of what can happen if you select funds based solely on annual lists of top performers. Many funds found at the top of these lists perform inconsistently; one year they're doing phenomenally well and the next year they're near the bottom. The frequent volatility of superstar funds often means they take greater risks to achieve their periodically outstanding returns. And risk is one factor that many fund "buy" lists ignore.

Prior to purchasing shares of any fund, you should understand what you are buying. There are hundreds of funds from which to choose, and there are wide differences between them. Funds differ in objective and in level of risk. There are mutual funds that can help you meet a growth objective and funds that can provide you with income. There are funds that combine growth and income objectives. Yet there are further distinctions between funds within these categories. Not all growth funds invest in the same kinds of stocks. Not all income funds invest in the same kinds of bonds. The differences in a fund's investments will affect a fund's returns and its level of risk.

Types of Mutual Funds

Before you can begin sorting through the many mutual funds available, you need to know more about your choices. Mutual funds are divided into two general categories – growth and income. For the most part, growth funds invest primarily in stocks and aim for capital appreciation. Income funds invest mainly in debt instruments – corporate and government bonds – and generate dividend income. Funds that combine growth and income invest in a broader mix of stocks and bonds.

A stock or bond fund's net asset value will fluctuate. The share price of a stock fund will cycle up and down with the broad market. The share price of a bond fund will fluctuate in relation to the value of the bonds held in the fund.

The following fund descriptions will tell you more about the fundamental differences between the various mutual funds and will help you better understand some of the building blocks of Diversified Mutual Fund Investing.

GROWTH FUNDS

Growth or stock funds still account for a large portion of all mutual fund assets. Common stocks are a good investment for capital appreciation and stock mutual funds offer investors an opportunity to take advantage of the higher profit potential of the market at a reduced risk. Your level of risk in stock funds will depend on which funds you select. Good stock funds will produce solid returns in up markets and remain relatively stable in down markets.

Generally widely diversified, a single stock fund will hold a large number of stocks. The total return from a stock fund is based on the fund's dividend and capital appreciation, which will be reflected in the changes in the fund's net asset value. Capital gains are realized when the fund sells stocks and other securities that have increased in value since their purchase. Shareholders receive these gains through distributions.

Aggressive Growth/Maximum Capital Appreciation Funds

Aggressive growth funds invest primarily in stocks of companies that have a high potential for rapid growth and maximum capital appreciation, sometimes with a secondary emphasis on dividend income. They often invest aggressively in smaller or newer fast-growing companies. These funds may trade actively, buy on margin, write options or use other speculative strategies. In their pursuit of maximum capital appreciation, aggressive growth funds are prepared to give up dividends and accept potentially volatile share prices.

Small Company Growth Funds

Small company growth funds emphasize rapid and long-term growth. They invest in the stock of small but growing companies. Stock in these companies has a high appreciation potential. Historically, small company stocks have provided the highest long-term returns. However, these stocks can also be very volatile.

Large Company Growth Funds

Long-term capital appreciation is the objective of large company growth funds. These funds invest in established companies with proven track records, good long-term earnings, steady growth and a high potential for continued results. Large company growth funds invest between 90 percent and 95 percent of their portfolio in stocks of companies whose earnings are expected to grow significantly faster than those of the S&P 500. While their investments include smaller companies that have greater growth potential and risk, they concentrate on major companies in an attempt to achieve consistent, above-average performance.

Equity Income Funds

The primary objective of equity income funds is to maximize income; growth of principal is secondary. Equity income funds invest in convertible bonds and stocks that pay high dividends. Normally at least half of the fund's assets are invested in common stocks that produce above-average returns. These funds offer investors the potential for greater capital gains over time than are possible with fixed-income funds. While the income from bond funds remains fixed, the dividends from equity income funds can increase or decrease.

Growth & Income Funds

Growth and income funds invest in both stocks and bonds. They aim for a nearly equal emphasis on income and long-term growth. They invest in common and preferred stocks, with the balance invested in government bonds, corporate bonds and cash equivalents.

This mix provides relatively high cash dividends along with the potential for capital appreciation.

International Stock Funds

International funds invest exclusively in foreign equity securities primarily for long-term growth. They invest in stocks of firms listed on the stock markets of foreign countries and regions. Fund performance is based on strong foreign economies in relation to a falling U.S. dollar.

Global Stock Funds

Global stock funds divide their holdings between U.S. and foreign securities and are structured to take advantage of markets around the world. They invest in foreign and domestic stocks for long-term growth and are typically less risky than strictly international funds since they are diversified worldwide and have less currency risk.

Option Income Funds

Option income funds invest primarily in stocks that pay steady dividends in an attempt to provide high income as an alternative to bonds. They do, however, frequently write options against those same stocks to supplement the dividend income and improve fund performance. If the options are called, there is the possibility that the fund's stocks will be sold at a loss, which will also cause the fund's shares to lose value.

Specialty/Sector Funds

Specialty funds, also called sector funds, concentrate their investments in a single industry, area of the market or geographic region. These funds are narrowly focused and tend to be very volatile. Sector funds include funds that invest in technology, gold or precious metals, automotive, finance, health, energy and natural resources and utilities. These funds usually invest in common stocks of high-quality companies showing a potential for sharp capital gains. Long-term growth is a common objective, although current dividend income may be sought.

Technology funds primarily hold common stocks of technological companies. Their holdings can include companies specializing in computers, satellite communications or robotics.

Gold/precious metals funds concentrate on the stock of companies involved primarily in mining and refining gold. Some holdings may be in gold bullion or companies that mine other precious metals. These funds seek speculative maximum capital gains plus some current income.

Automotive funds invest in a variety of automotive-related industries that include manufacturers and parts suppliers.

Finance funds invest mostly in the equities of financial companies, among which are banks, insurance companies and brokerage firms.

Health funds hold equity positions in a variety of health care companies, including hospitals, hospital equipment manufacturers, drug companies and biotechnology firms.

Energy and natural resource funds invest more than half of their assets in companies producing or distributing natural resources, or energy and related products and equipment – oil, gas, coal, forest products, mineral mines and resource development.

Utility funds include the securities of companies that manufacture, generate, transmit and sell gas and electric energy and companies specializing in telephone, telegraph and satellite communications.

INCOME FUNDS

Income funds invest most of their assets in bonds and other fixed-income securities. Investing in a bond mutual fund reduces the risks of buying individual bonds while it provides income. Although bonds are the most consistent way to achieve steady income, they are not without their own risk. Longer-maturing bonds, in particular, are more subject to interest rate fluctuations. Interest rates will influence the value of bonds held in a fund and will be reflected in the fund's net asset value. Lower-quality bonds also present a greater risk of default.

Taxable Fixed-Income Funds

Fixed-income funds typically invest in government or corporate bonds, cash instruments and occasionally preferred and high-dividend stocks. These funds provide shareholders with taxable income in the form of dividends.

Corporate Bond Funds

Corporate bond funds seek current income through investments in taxable fixed-income securities. Although the quality and maturity of securities purchased by corporate bond funds varies, these funds primarily purchase corporate obligations with maturities of at least one year. They tend to pay higher rates than government bond funds, but they also present a greater risk of default.

General Corporate Bond Funds

General corporate bond funds invest in various fixed-income securities – mostly corporate bonds of varying quality – purchased primarily for income.

High-Quality Corporate Bond Funds

High-quality corporate bond funds, also known as high-grade corporate funds, invest primarily in highly-rated bonds to provide interest income.

High-Yield Corporate Bond Funds

High-yield corporate bond funds seek to maximize income by investing most of their assets in lower-quality corporate bonds. These funds may also invest in junk bonds – high-yielding, long-term issues that are generally considered to be below investment grade.

U.S. Government Bond Funds

U.S. Government bond funds invest only in debt issues of the U.S. Treasury or government agencies. These funds have provided a slightly lower historical rate of return than corporate bond funds. Their investments include bonds, bills and notes issued by the government or agencies of the government.

General Government Bond Funds

General government bond funds invest in U.S. Government issues or issues of government agencies, along with some mortgage-backed securities.

Government Mortgage-Backed Bond Funds

Government mortgage-backed bond funds invest more than half of their assets in Government National Mortgage Association (GNMA) securities. GNMA securities are government-backed mortgages bought from banks and savings and loans. They combine the features of bonds and mortgages and provide investors with monthly payments of interest and principal. Many GNMA funds balance their positions by purchasing other fixed-income government securities.

Government Treasury Bond Funds

Government Treasury bond funds invest more than three-fourths of their assets in U.S. Treasury securities. U.S. Treasury securities have the highest credit rating.

International Bond Funds

International bond funds invest in bonds issued by foreign governments and corporations. They may also invest in the securities of a particular country or region.

Global Bond Funds

Global bond funds invest in foreign and domestic stocks and bonds for capital appreciation and income. They profit not only from the growth and income of their securities, but from currency transactions and potential capital gains opportunities.

Tax-Free Income Funds — Municipal Bond Funds

Municipal bond funds invest in a broad range of short-term and long-term securities issued by municipalities. State, city and other local governments issue bonds to help them raise money. The objective of municipal bond funds is tax-free income for investors. Earnings from these funds are exempt from federal income tax; they are also exempt from state and local taxes in the state in which the bonds were issued. The quality and maturities of these fund holdings vary.

Insured Municipal Bond Funds

Insured municipal bond funds purchase only insured tax-free bonds. These are high-quality municipal bonds. The bonds are insured so that if they do default, the loss is covered.

High-Yield Municipal Bond Funds

High-yield municipal bond funds buy lower-quality municipal bonds for maximum income. This type of bond is subject to a much greater risk of default than any other type of municipal bond.

General Municipal Bond Funds

General municipal bond funds invest in bonds that vary in credit quality. These funds may purchase bonds that range from a AAA rating to a BBB rating.

HYBRID FUNDS

Hybrid funds are those funds that do not fit exclusively in either the growth or income category. Their objective is some combination of growth and income, as they tend to invest in different proportions of both stocks and bonds.

Asset Allocation Funds

Asset allocation funds try to blend stocks, bonds, cash and sometimes gold and foreign stocks to preserve principal and achieve capital gains. Fund holdings will vary. These funds often shift actively between different types of investments, placing a priority on securities that are currently in favor. They aim for the best returns from each asset category.

Convertible Bond Funds

Convertible bond funds invest mostly in bonds and preferred stocks that can be converted into a specified number of shares of a company's common stock. Possessing the features of both stocks and bonds, convertible bond funds provide fixed income and the potential for capital gains.

You've seen the types of funds available to you as an investor. You can invest in funds that hold stocks in small companies, large companies or special areas of the market for capital appreciation. You can invest in funds holding corporate bonds, government bonds or tax-free bonds to produce different levels of income. You can also invest in funds that hold both stocks and bonds for a combination of income and capital appreciation. But that's just the start. There is much more information you will need to analyze before you can confidently select funds for your portfolio.

FUND INVESTMENT STRATEGY AND MANAGEMENT

Return and risk are the most important fund performance factors to consider when selecting mutual funds. As they are primary to Diversified Mutual Fund Investing, return and risk will be covered in the next chapter. Yet return and risk are not the only factors you will need to assess. There are other internal fund variables that can affect a fund's performance which should be analyzed when determining a fund's investment potential.

Two of those other fund variables are a fund's investment strategy and the fund manager's implementation of that strategy. Although these two variables can both influence a fund's performance, many investors don't pay enough attention to them.

Has the fund's investment strategy been implemented consistently? You want to make certain, for example, that a fund with a conservative growth objective will not be purchasing stock options. How flexible is the fund's strategy? A manager will have less influence on a fund that has a more rigid investment strategy, while a fund with a more flexible investment strategy will allow the manager more discretion in making investment decisions.

Other than market movements, much of a fund's performance is closely tied to the decisions made by the fund's manager; it is the manager who can be the determining factor in a fund's success or failure. Remember, when you invest in a mutual fund, you're buying the fund's manager along with your shares. This is the person or team who will be implementing the fund's strategy and controlling your money. Who is responsible for the fund's day-to-day operations? Who makes the decisions? Sometimes determining exactly who manages a fund is no easy task as fund managers are often not very visible. You may well have to call the fund to obtain that information.

If the fund is directed by one person, a practice frequently referred to as the "star" system, you need to know something about the manager's experience. How long has the manager been with the fund? Some funds have trouble retaining key people. If the fund's manager has changed, a fund's superior performance history may be irrelevant because past performance would not reflect the skills of the current manager. In such a case, you should place less emphasis on earlier returns and focus primarily on the returns attributable to the new manager. You could also check on the performance of other funds or accounts this person has managed.

If a team is managing a fund, you need to know something about the main players. What are their responsibilities? Do they manage the fund full-time or part-time? How long have they been part of the team? When a team manages a fund, it's more difficult to determine exactly who is responsible for fund performance. And like anything else managed by committee, compromises may be made that are not always best for the fund or investors. A fund organization may even move fund managers between funds within the fund family.

While a fund with a long and stable performance record is a stronger fund for your consideration, you shouldn't necessarily ignore new funds, either. If the fund's manager is a person with proven abilities and a solid track record, the fund may indeed be a suitable choice for your portfolio. Consistently strong, long-term fund performance, achieved over market highs and lows, is a reflection of a fund manager's abilities. While you can't assume the fund will do well in the future because it did so in the past, this type of performance is a good indication of a skillful fund manager.

MANAGEMENT APPROACHES

How does a fund manager evaluate and select stocks or bonds for the fund? How much emphasis does the manager place on the economy versus individual company strengths?

Funds can employ different strategies to achieve their objectives. Likewise fund managers differ in their investment approaches or the way they intend to pursue a fund's stated objective. The investment approach that is applied depends on the fund manager and the manager's style. All managers have a preferred method for analyzing data and determining what they should buy and sell for the fund's portfolio, yet they tend to follow two basic types of approaches to investment analysis – a "top-down" or "bottom-up" approach. There are also managers who follow their own unique or "eclectic" approach, which is generally some combination of top-down and bottom-up analysis.

Top-Down Analysis

Investment strategists who follow top-down investment analysis are most concerned with macroeconomic variables. They begin their analysis with the economy, both domestic and international, and work their way down through the stock and bond markets, sectors of the market and then industries before making specific security selections. Their main interest, however, is in what the overall economy is doing and how the economy interacts with business.

To gain an understanding of the economy, these strategists study a wide range of economic reports and statistics. Looking for relationships and patterns, they analyze various economic components, current economic events and business activity. They reason that by understanding the data, they can determine in which direction the economy and thus business is headed; if the economy does well, the stock market will also do well.

Like many parts of our lives, the economy follows cyclical patterns. As the economy expands and then contracts, there are corresponding fluctuations in business activity. This up-and-down pattern is known as the "business cycle." Top-down strategists pay close attention to the business cycle because it reflects economic activity. When the economy prospers, the business cycle moves up. When the economy takes a downturn, the business cycle will also dip.

Top-down strategists also study factors within the economic system that they consider to be signs of economic expansion or contraction. These indicators include bank lending patterns, the money supply, interest rates, federal fiscal policy, the Gross National Product, foreign exchange rates, the International Monetary Fund, the balance of trade, inflation measures, the stock market and the Dow Jones Industrial Average, industrial production, company profits and business expenditures. Some of the consumer-related factors which top-down strategists study are demand, the Consumer Price Index and the Index of Consumer Sentiment.

Bottom-Up Analysis

Bottom-up analysts pay little attention to economic factors. Instead, they concentrate on a company's stock. They study available data to understand, as thoroughly

as possible, how a company operates and to draw con-
clusions about the company's potential for profit. Former
Fidelity Magellan Fund manager Peter Lynch has said
he has no use for market forecasters, economists or
interest rate predictions. He also has said he does not
pay much attention to market volatility. At Magellan,
Lynch focused solely on long-term company prospects.
It's a strategy that has paid off well for the Magellan
Fund, one of the best performing funds in history.

Likewise, many of the best fund managers aren't
concerned about what the economy or interest rates are
going to do because they know they can't predict or
control either one. What they can do is make judgments
about risks and rewards based on individual company
strengths and weaknesses. They look for companies
that will perform well regardless of the economy; they
believe that a good company is still inherently a good
company despite high interest rates or a weak dollar.
Their goal is to find strong companies with underval-
ued shares that can be sold later at a profit.

A large number of company variables are analyzed
when making decisions about a company's appropri-
ateness for a fund's portfolio. Bottom-up analysts study
a company's financial statements and take into account
all of a company's characteristics and business activities
to assist them in determining the value of a company's
securities independent of the market. What is the stock
really worth? What is the fair market value based on
assets, sales, cash flow, earnings, dividends, future
prospects and management? Bottom-up analysts ap-
praise the risk factors associated with company products,

the competition and debt. Key ratios are used as part of the analysis to provide additional information about the company's overall performance, the safety of its securities and the attractiveness of its common stock. Bottom-up analysts often meet with a company's management and staff to see first-hand how the company operates. Based on these factors, bottom-up analysts make realistic assumptions about the trend of company growth and earnings, the stability of the company and the future value of its securities.

THE IMPACT OF LOADS

Fund loads, and how they affect your returns, are another factor you should consider when making your fund selections. Should you invest in load funds or only in no-loads? That depends.

Fund loads and expenses can eat up a substantial portion of your return if they are excessive. From a long-term perspective, however, fund performance is far more important than a load. Too many people focus exclusively on loads when evaluating funds even though other performance factors are of greater consequence.

Usually loads are taken out of your purchase before your money is invested in the fund. If you consider the power of compounding, a front-end load may have a greater effect on your investment than you might expect. A front-end load is not simply a percentage taken out up-front, but a percentage that remains lost for as long as you hold the investment.

Compare the two $10,000 fund purchases in Figure 10. One investment is made in a no-load fund and the other is in a fund with an 8.5 percent front-end load. You can see the difference the up-front load makes on your return over a 10-year period assuming a 10% annual rate of return.

Figure 10

Effect of a Front-End Load on a $10,000 Investment

	No-Load Fund	8.5% Load Fund
Initial investment	$10,000	$10,000
Load	0	– $850
Net investment	$10,000	$9,150
1 Year	$11,000	$10,065
2 Years	$12,100	$11,071
3 Years	$13,310	$12,179
4 Years	$14,641	$13,397
5 Years	$16,105	$14,736
6 Years	$17,716	$16,210
7 Years	$19,487	$17,831
8 Years	$21,436	$19,614
9 Years	$23,579	$21,575
10 Years	$25,937	$23,733

As Figure 10 shows, if you invest in the fund with the load, only $9,150 of your money is put to work for you, so you start off at a disadvantage. The gap that is apparent from the beginning only widens as each year passes. After 10 years, the difference on your return is $2,204.

What about a front-end load versus a back-end load? If a back-end load or redemption fee were charged only on your principal, it would cost you less than a front-end load. But a back-end load is subtracted from the entire amount of your investment. Many investors may find it hard to believe, but as Figure 11 shows, paying a front-end load actually has the same effect as paying a back-end load, or deferred sales charge, on your entire investment.

Figure 11

Effects of a Front-End Load Versus a Back-End Load

	Front-End Load Fund	Back-End Load Fund
Initial investment	$10,000.00	$10,000.00
Front-end 4% load	− $400.00	0
Net investment	$ 9,600.00	$10,000.00
Investment after 6 years at 8%	$15,233.99	$15,868.74
Back-end 4% load on entire investment	0	− $ 634.75
Value upon withdrawal	$15,233.99	$15,233.99

If you begin with a $10,000 investment and pay a 4 percent front-end load, your net investment is $9,600.00. After six years, if your investment earns 8 percent, it will be worth $15,233.99. If you invest $10,000 in a fund with a full, deferred sales charge, your entire $10,000 would be invested initially. After six years at an average of 8 percent per year, your investment would be worth $15,868.74. But if you chose to withdraw your money at that point and had to pay the 4 percent back-end load on your principal and earnings, your net would also be $15,233.99.

Keep in mind that a fund's published total return figures include management fees and operating expenses, but they often do not reflect the impact of loads or redemption charges. If you pay either a load or a redemption charge on your fund shares, your actual return will be less than the published results. Take a look at the top performing funds and factor in any loads that apply. Are the funds still top performers?

Profitable investing means earning the highest risk-adjusted total return possible. That usually means you are better off starting with every cent of your money invested in a fund. If all other fund variables are equal, you should stick with no-load funds for your portfolio. The only real difference between loads and no-loads is the commission that goes to the broker and his or her firm; a commission does not buy you better research or better fund management. Purchasing shares in a load fund can, however, provide you with investment advice from the person who is selling you the fund, which can be beneficial. On the other hand, professional asset management services can also be worth every dollar they cost you in fees if the asset manager helps you earn a higher return on your investment than you could on your own.

There may be times, however, when you will want to consider buying shares of a load fund. Although it doesn't happen very often, it is possible that a load fund could outperform a no-load. A load fund may, for example, have an outstanding manager. Investors who skip over a fund simply because it is a load fund could miss an opportunity. So you cannot necessarily rule out *all* funds that have a load. If you are convinced that a load fund is an exceptional performer, the load will matter less over time. Weigh all of the factors carefully before you decide to invest in a load fund and make certain you will be well compensated for paying the load.

The Prospectus

As part of your fund analysis, you should assess more specific information about the funds you are considering. Much of what you need to know will be found in the fund's prospectus. You may also find pertinent fund information in a fund's separate Form B, or Statement of Additional Information, if the fund has one. While fund documents contain quite a bit of data, you should pay the closest attention to several key items: investment performance and per share data, investment objectives and fund strategy, portfolio composition and fees and expenses.

INVESTMENT PERFORMANCE AND PER SHARE DATA

Fund documents will show you the returns the fund has earned over the past several years, making it easier to evaluate the fund in relation to the market. Did the fund perform better or worse than the market as a whole? You should look at annual returns over the last 10 years, if the fund has been in existence that long.

Take a look at the fund's price per share. Has it changed radically from quarter to quarter, or has it been consistent and stable? While the price in and of itself is not a concern, changes in the share price will not only show you how well the fund performed, but will tell you something about the fund's volatility. A volatile fund will have more rapid price changes and greater risk.

INVESTMENT OBJECTIVES AND FUND STRATEGY

The prospectus will explain how the fund intends to pursue its investment objective. Mutual funds must clearly state their objectives in the prospectus and must also adhere to them. Some prospectuses use vague language to describe a fund's objective or strategy. If you cannot clearly understand a fund's investment objective or strategy by what you read in the prospectus, call the fund and ask questions. If your questions are not answered satisfactorily, maybe you should reconsider the fund as a prospect for your portfolio.

PORTFOLIO COMPOSITION

Take a look at where the fund has its money. What percentage of fund assets is in stocks or bonds? Look at the kinds of stocks and bonds in the fund's portfolio. They will tell you something about the fund's risk level. Look at the maturities and credit ratings of the bonds held. Most bond funds hold bonds with an average 10-year maturity. A fund holding many long-term bonds paying higher rates of interest may be more susceptible to losses if interest rates rise.

How fully is the fund invested? How much of the fund's assets are in cash? The answers to these questions will tell you how optimistic or pessimistic the fund's manager is about the market. How widely are the fund's assets distributed? What are the largest holdings in the fund's portfolio? Looking at these points will also tell you something about the fund's diversification and investment strategy. If two funds are supposed to follow different strategies, but they invest in similar securities, how different are they really?

FEES AND EXPENSES

As of May 1988, funds must identify all fees and expenses charged to shareholders. They must also include a table in the prospectus clearly indicating how any fees, expenses and sales charges will affect an investment over various time periods. This information makes it easier for investors to compare fund costs.

The only way you can learn how much is taken out of the fund's profits for fees and expenses is by studying the prospectus. Management fees, overhead and any 12b-1 charges are added together and shown as an annual expense ratio, or expenses as a percentage of average net assets. Notice whether there are high sales charges or other costs that will affect your return or limit the proportion of your investment going into the fund.

How much weight should you place on a fund's fees or expenses? In order to decide, you need to know the extent to which fees and expenses affect a fund's returns. Returns are still the bottom line, along with volatility and fund management. If a fund performs well, providing a stable, higher return, a slightly higher expense ratio should not make enough of a difference for you to totally disregard the fund. But if you're considering two funds that are very much alike except that one has higher fees, you should of course select the fund with lower fees.

Besides the key factors relating to a fund that have already been mentioned, there are several other variables you should take a look at. They may or may not be as important, but they still merit some attention.

FUND SIZE

Too many investors become overconcerned with the size of a fund. Not a single academic study concludes that a smaller fund is better than a larger fund. As fund assets grow, expenses per share usually drop because they can be spread over a wider asset base. Transaction costs can also be reduced because larger funds tend to trade in larger blocks of stock. But funds that are too large can be more challenging to manage. The particular fund and the manager's performance are still the most important considerations. It's the results that count.

FUNDS WITHIN A FAMILY

Families of funds were created to provide investors with extra diversification while keeping investor dollars within the same investment company. You can, for example, hold both income and growth funds within many fund groups. But holding several of these funds may not provide the same level of diversification as selecting funds in completely different families. Although each fund may have a different manager, funds within a family tend to have many similarities. Sometimes funds within a family are no more than variations of the same investment approach. Fund managers within a family often share investment ideas that are reflected in their accounts.

FUND TURNOVER

A fund's turnover, or turnover ratio, is a measure of trading activity. It will tell you how frequently the fund's mix of securities changes. Changes in a fund's turnover ratio can also indicate changes in a fund's management approach.

A fund's turnover rate is calculated by dividing fund purchases or sales (whichever is less) by average monthly fund assets. A higher turnover of fund holdings can increase a fund's transaction costs and, in turn, fund expenses. Although a lower turnover ratio is preferable, whether or not a high fund turnover is a problem depends on how it affects a fund's returns. If a fund manager achieves high risk-adjusted returns over time with a high portfolio turnover rate, it should not be viewed as a problem.

Now that you've seen the factors that can affect a fund's performance, how can you narrow down the many funds available to a manageable number of choices? More specifically, how do you go about building a Diversified Mutual Fund portfolio? There is a process you can use that will help you structure your portfolio to reach your investment objective. And there is a specific methodology you can follow to select individual mutual funds that will provide you with the highest returns at the lowest risk. That's what you'll learn in the next chapter.

Chapter 4

Building a Diversified Portfolio of Mutual Funds

A portfolio that can meet your investment objective and produce the highest returns with the lowest level of risk over the long term. Sound too good to be true?

Diversified Mutual Fund Investing can be profitable for all investors. Regardless of your investment objective, or the amount you wish to invest, you can build your own portfolio of funds that will provide you with the best returns possible at the lowest relative level of risk. You can achieve these results efficiently and cost-effectively by selecting, buying and holding a diverse number of funds that are proven high performers on a risk-adjusted basis.

But it takes more than simply investing in a number of funds to provide you with true diversification and safety. It takes the strengths of a variety of fund managers and funds from different asset categories combined within a single portfolio. The proper mix of fund managers and asset categories can decrease your risk without reducing your profit potential.

Following the Diversified Mutual Fund Investing process will enable you to easily integrate the expertise of a number of professional money managers within a single portfolio. Each mutual fund you select will have its own manager who has a distinctive investment approach. Each manager also has a style of investing that influences the fund's performance over time. Although many investment styles will produce good returns over the long-term, a particular style may not fare as well in the short-term. Thus, your portfolio's performance should be based on the skills of a diverse group of investment professionals. Investing in funds whose managers have contrasting styles will help you avoid lower short-term returns.

You need to select enough funds so that your portfolio's performance will not be dependent on too few funds and fund managers. A portfolio with five funds, for example, provides you with the investment expertise of five unique fund managers. If three of the five funds you have selected perform poorly, your entire portfolio will not be adversely affected.

Diversified Mutual Fund Investing also makes it easy for you to integrate funds from different asset categories, with varying levels of risk, within a single portfolio. Investments in the growth, income and liquid asset categories will produce dissimilar patterns of returns. Funds within each of these categories will also produce returns at varying levels of risk. Your combination of asset categories and funds within these categories will determine your overall risk as well as your return. Holding funds in different categories and with diverse levels of risk will help stabilize your portfolio's performance.

THE PROCESS

The Diversified Mutual Fund Investing process is similar to the process you would use to put together a portfolio of individual securities. If you build your own portfolio using individual stocks and bonds, however, you really are performing two separate functions: You are the portfolio manager and the security selector.

As the portfolio manager you must structure your portfolio between asset categories. You have to decide how you should allocate your assets to best meet your investment objective of growth, income, or some combination. Should you place your assets primarily in stocks or bonds? In what proportions? Should you invest in aggressive or conservative stocks? Should you use bonds or high-dividend stock investments for income?

When you build your own portfolio, you are also the security selector. Based on your asset allocation, you must analyze data to carefully select individual stocks or bonds that will meet your investment objective. And with the many alternatives available, that is a formidable task.

The functions of portfolio management and security selection each require time and expertise. Each of the functions can also be performed more effectively if it is separated from the other. Diversified Mutual Fund Investing splits those tasks.

In Diversified Mutual Fund Investing you will remain the portfolio manager and decide how to allocate your assets. You will determine whether you should be primarily in stock, bond or money market investments and in what proportions. However, you will no longer select individual securities. Instead, you will select a group of mutual funds and mutual fund managers who will perform this function. The mutual fund managers will pick individual stocks and bonds for the funds' portfolios; it will be up to them to meet the funds' investment objectives, and in turn, yours. Fund managers are experienced investment professionals who spend most of their time concentrating solely on selecting securities. They also have the research staffs they need to help them make informed decisions.

Following the Diversified Mutual Fund Investing process can only increase the probability that you will invest profitably; it will allow you to invest in the stock and bond markets at a lower risk than you could on your own. If you select funds properly, you won't have to be as concerned with the risk of inflation. You will find stock funds that are less likely to be severely affected by a downturn in the market than your own stock selections might be. And you will find bond funds that are less subject to credit risk than the individual bonds you might select on your own.

By now you are aware that there is much more to Diversified Mutual Fund Investing than narrowing your choices down to 10 funds and simply picking six. Diversified Mutual Fund Investing is a process you can follow first to structure your portfolio, giving you a base on which to build. Then you can use Diversified Mutual Fund Investing's fund selection strategy to help you pick stock and bond funds that will meet your investment objective. As a combination of statistical fund analysis and informed judgment, this method will assist you in choosing top performing funds while eliminating those funds that take excessive risk.

You can build your own Diversified Mutual Fund portfolio by following the three-step process shown in Figure 12. Notice that each step builds upon the other. You begin by determining your investment objective, move on to asset allocation, and then select individual funds for your portfolio. Each step will be covered in greater detail shortly.

Figure 12

Diversified Mutual Fund Investing

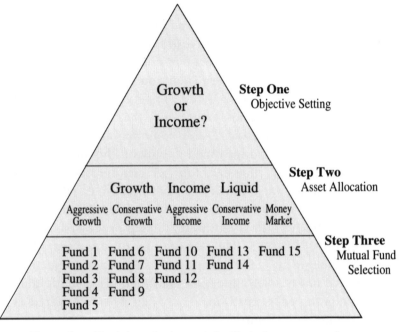

The number of funds in each category is for illustrative purposes only.

SAVINGS VERSUS INVESTMENT DOLLARS

Before you invest any of your money, you need to take a good look at your situation. What are your current financial obligations? How much cash is required to meet your liquidity needs? Answering these questions will help you determine how much money you should keep liquid as savings and how much is available for investing.

Your savings and investment dollars should not be confused; each serves an independent function. Your savings is a liquid cash reserve, money you have access to for your day-to-day needs and any emergency situation that might arise. It is money that should be kept as risk-free as possible. You should set aside a sufficient amount of money in savings before you make any investments. You don't want to have to liquidate one of your investments at the wrong time if you should need immediate cash.

There are many ways you can keep your savings dollars liquid. You can set up a checking or a savings account, or put your money in a bank money market account. But a good alternative to these savings vehicles is a money market mutual fund. Like other mutual funds, money market funds pool the money of many investors. They were created in the 1970s to give small investors the opportunity to obtain the higher rates of return that were once available only to larger investors who purchased Treasury bills and commercial paper.

Bank money market accounts and money market mutual funds both invest in short-term debt consisting of U.S. Treasury bills, government agency obligations, certificates of deposit, commercial or corporate paper (short-term debt issued by corporations), banker's acceptances (short-term discount notes arising out of foreign trade transactions), repurchase agreements (very short-term loans) and Eurodollar certificates. These are investments that mature in one year or less. Investing in such short-term debt allows money market accounts and money market mutual funds to maintain safety of principal and a net asset value of $1 per share.

Bank money market accounts and money market mutual funds allow you to withdraw money at any time by simply writing a check or making a phone call. However, money market funds may require higher minimum deposits than a bank money market account.

Nevertheless, money market mutual funds do offer advantages over bank money market accounts. Money market funds are professionally managed and diversified. They seek maximum return to the extent they can still maintain stability of principal, earning interest at a rate that fluctuates daily yet is generally slightly higher than the rate on bank savings or bank money market accounts. Although money market funds may invest in debt instruments guaranteed by the federal government, the funds themselves are investment companies and thus are not guaranteed. Bank money markets, on the other hand, are government insured; for this added security they typically earn a lower rate of return.

There are several different types of money market mutual funds, which vary in the paper (debt) they purchase — regular money market funds, government money market funds, prime funds and tax-free funds.

Regular money market funds, or general funds, buy obligations of the U.S. Government and its agencies, CDs, banker's acceptances, and investments in highly-rated corporate paper, examples of which are bonds, debentures, notes and repurchase agreements.

Government money market funds invest only in U.S. Government securities – Treasury bills, notes, bonds and other obligations issued or guaranteed by the U.S. Government and its agencies and repurchase agreements of such obligations. Government money market funds pay a slightly lower rate of return than regular money market funds.

Prime money market funds invest only in the highest-quality money market instruments. Prime fund purchases include government debt instruments and high-quality commercial paper.

Tax-free money market funds buy short-term, high-quality municipal paper. They provide lower returns than the other money market funds, but the dividends from these funds are exempt from federal income tax; you may still have to pay state and local taxes.

Another reason a money market fund is a good place to put your savings dollars or temporarily park your money is that there are no charges for deposits or withdrawals and your principal remains stable. You can find the rates for money market funds listed weekly in many newspapers. While money market funds pay higher rates than bank money market accounts, those rates are about even with or only a little above the inflation rate, so you're not really getting ahead. When taxes are paid on the interest that is earned and inflation is factored in, money market funds rarely provide positive real rates of return.

Yet as these funds provide an attractive alternative

to bank accounts for savings, money market funds are a convenient way to keep a designated portion of your investment dollars liquid. A small allotment of your portfolio should remain liquid not only to help balance your portfolio, but to enable you to take advantage of investment opportunities that arise; it will give you easy access to your money if you need it for investment purposes. Because money market funds are so similar, there is little need for diversification; one money market fund is generally sufficient to fulfill your portfolio's liquidity and safety requirements.

DETERMINING YOUR INVESTMENT OBJECTIVE

Now that you've set aside sufficient money in savings and have considered your liquidity, you're ready to move on to the first step in Diversified Mutual Fund Investing – determining your investment objective. This is the beginning of your financial strategy and will provide you with a starting point for financial success.

As Figure 13 shows, your investment objective comes down to one basic question – do you want to invest for growth, income, or a combination of the two?

Figure 13

Diversified Mutual Fund Investing

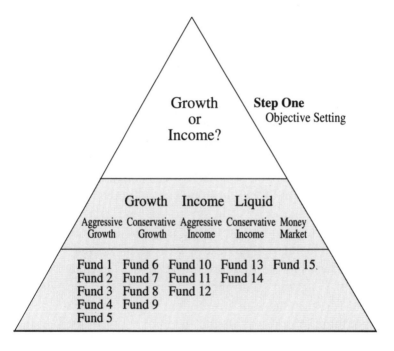

To help you determine which investment objective is most suitable for you to pursue, you need to assess your own financial situation and decide how you want your money to be working for you.

You can ask yourself the following questions:

• Do you have sufficient income and simply want to build upon your current assets?

• Do you need some income and want the potential for growth?

• Do you simply need income now?

Should you invest primarily for growth or income, or some combination of the two? If you have sufficient income for your current needs and you want to build upon your wealth, then your investment objective should be growth. The best way to meet your growth objective would be through stock funds. They will produce relatively little or no income, but they will provide the greatest potential for your assets to appreciate in value. Your return will be based on that appreciation, or the increase in the fund's net asset value.

If you need some income, but also want the potential for growth, your investment objective should be a combination of growth and income. Your objective, in this case, will best be met through a portfolio that is balanced between stock and bond funds.

If you need money for living expenses, your investment objective should be primarily income and you should structure your portfolio for that purpose. The most consistent way to meet your income objective would be through bond funds, which will provide you with interest income.

ASSET ALLOCATION

The most important consideration for your investment success is selecting the right asset category. The long-term performance of professionally managed money indicates that well over 90 percent of the results can be attributed solely to the asset categories selected; the specific securities have less of an effect on performance.

The principle of selecting the proper asset category also applies to Diversified Mutual Fund Investing. Thus, it is more important that you select the growth or income category, as appropriate, and less important which particular stock or bond funds you select. It is the broad performance difference between the stock and bond fund categories that will have the greatest impact on whether you achieve your investment objective.

Asset allocation is the second step in the Diversified Mutual Fund Investing process. Here, "asset allocation" simply means selecting the investment categories that will best meet your objective for growth or income. As you can see in Figure 14, Step Two in Diversified Mutual Fund Investing begins with dividing your investment dollars between the main asset categories – growth, income and liquid.

For growth investors the asset mix should consist of some combination of stock funds. Income investors need to allocate a greater proportion of their assets to income funds. Most investors should also keep a small portion of their portfolio liquid. A money market fund, as we have seen, is one easy way to maintain this liquidity. Remember that this liquid category is not savings; it is money to be kept available as a cash investment reserve. If you should choose to purchase additional fund shares in the future, dollars would be available from this liquid allocation.

Figure 14

Diversified Mutual Fund Investing

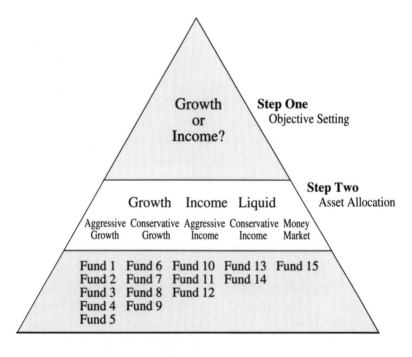

Once you have divided your assets among these major categories, you will need to further split your assets between types of fund groups – aggressive growth, conservative growth, aggressive income or conservative income.

Aggressive growth funds have historically provided higher rates of return and therefore have a greater potential for long-term appreciation, but they tend to be more volatile. Examples of aggressive growth funds are aggressive growth/maximum capital appreciation funds and small company growth funds. While conservative growth funds tend to be less volatile, historically they also have provided lower rates of return. Large company growth funds, equity income funds and growth and income funds are examples of conservative growth funds.

Similarly, income funds can be divided between aggressive and conservative income categories. The difference between aggressive and conservative income funds is in the quality of the bonds they hold and the resultant variations in market risk and credit risk. As with aggressive growth funds, aggressive income funds have historically tended to provide higher rates of return. They invest in bonds with lower credit quality. Aggressive income funds include general corporate bond funds, high-yield corporate bond funds and high-yield municipal bond funds. Conservative income funds, on the other hand, invest in higher-quality debt with little or no credit risk and have produced lower rates of return. High-quality corporate bond funds, U.S. Government bond funds and insured municipal bond funds are examples of conservative income funds.

YOUR RISK TOLERANCE

If you had to choose between two investments that paid the same return, you would most likely choose the one with lower risk. If you had to choose between two investments with the same level of risk, you'd no doubt choose the one paying the higher return. Seeking the highest returns with the lowest risk, is, of course, a prudent investment strategy.

How you decide to split your growth and income allocations between aggressive and conservative funds will first be determined by which type of assets will best meet your objective. But allocating your assets between aggressive and conservative funds will also depend upon the amount of risk you can assume. Not everyone is able or willing to take on greater risk, even though there may be an opportunity for greater profit. Your risk tolerance, or your ability and desire to assume risk, depends upon your financial situation and you as an individual.

Answering these questions will help you evaluate your own risk tolerance:

- Is the investment a vital part of your assets?

- Are you financially able to take a loss?

- How much of your investment can you afford to lose?

- Which is more important – maximum gain or safety of principal?

- What type of risk would be least detrimental to your own investment goals – market risk, default risk or inflation risk?

Despite promises of a higher return, many people are just not comfortable with an investment that entails greater risk. Investors also tend to be less comfortable with inconsistent returns. Suppose two investments have each earned 30 percent over three years. The first investment was up 11 percent one year, up 4 percent the next year and up 15 percent the third year. The other investment was up 15 percent the first year, down 8 percent the second year and up 23 percent the third year. Although both investments produced a 30 percent cumulative return, most investors would perceive the more stable returns of the first investment as being easier to live with.

There are plenty of mutual funds that will provide you with an opportunity for profit without requiring that you take on unnecessary risk. Assuming excessive risk is not a guarantee of higher returns, but it does increase your chance of sustaining a loss. And once you experience a loss, making up for it and getting back on track is extremely difficult. If you lose 20 percent of your investment, you need to earn 25 percent to make up for it; if you suffer a 50 percent loss, you need a 100 percent gain just to break even.

A PORTFOLIO BASED ON YOUR INVESTMENT NEEDS

Your portfolio should be structured to provide you with a strategy that will meet your current investment objective within your risk tolerance. Yet deciding to invest for growth, income, or some combination of the two does not mean your portfolio will retain the same structure forever. Your investment objective and your resultant asset allocation can, and most likely will, change over time as your needs for growth or income change. There are certain periods in a person's life when there is a greater emphasis on growth and accumulating assets. If income is needed at some point, a growth objective can be shifted and assets can be reallocated into investments which will produce income.

It is often assumed that when an investor is young, growth is most important and should be pursued aggressively. It is also assumed that later, during retirement, the emphasis should be placed on income. While it is true that as an investor approaches retirement there is generally a greater emphasis on security, your investment objective does not have to change simply because you retire. You may begin as a growth investor and you may not require additional income at any point in your life. What is more likely to change is your risk tolerance. Investors often become more conservative with their money as they age.

You can control the amount of risk within a specific asset category by allocating a greater proportion of your assets to either conservative or aggressive growth or income funds. You could maintain a growth objective, but you may decide to pursue it more conservatively. Or you may begin as a conservative growth investor and become more aggressive as you become more financially secure. Likewise, you may be an investor who chooses to pursue an income objective in either a more conservative or aggressive manner over time.

The following sample portfolios will illustrate how asset allocation can shift in response to shifts in investment objective and risk tolerance. You will notice that there are not only distinctions between growth and income, but whether an income or growth objective is being pursued aggressively or conservatively.

Figure 15 shows how a portfolio could be allocated for maximum growth. This portfolio represents an investor who doesn't need investment income currently, so the primary objective is to build capital. Maximum growth indicates that a more aggressive approach is being taken to achieve the greatest growth possible. Yet such a growth portfolio would also entail assuming greater risk in the form of market volatility.

A maximum growth portfolio typically belongs to a relatively young investor who can withstand short-term market fluctuations in exchange for the greater long-term growth opportunities often provided by stocks. Even though the market can be volatile in the short-term, stocks have historically produced the highest long-term gains. If income should be needed at some later point, this investor would also have a greater capital base from which to produce that income.

Figure 15

A Maximum Growth Portfolio

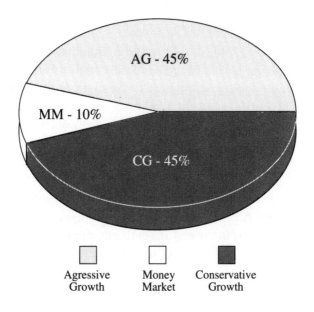

Agressive
Growth

Money
Market

Conservative
Growth

This is just one example of how a maximum growth portfolio
could be allocated.

This maximum growth portfolio has 90 percent of
the assets allocated to growth funds and 10 percent
kept liquid in a money market fund. The growth allocation is split evenly between aggressive growth and
conservative growth. The aggressive allocation represents funds having a higher growth potential and greater

volatility; they would likely provide higher returns but also add risk to the portfolio. Allocating 45 percent of the portfolio to conservative growth funds would provide a lower but more consistent level of growth; it would also help stabilize the portfolio's overall returns and lower the overall risk.

Once this investor has a money market fund for liquidity, he could choose 10 mutual funds for his maximum growth portfolio. The aggressive growth selections could include a couple of small company growth funds, a couple of aggressive growth/maximum capital appreciation funds, two specialty/sector funds and one international fund. Two large company growth funds and an equity income fund could be sufficient for the conservative growth portion of the portfolio. For this investor it is more important to diversify among the aggressive funds than the conservative because the former have greater volatility.

You can also take a more conservative approach to growth investing. Figure 16 represents a more conservative growth portfolio. This investor still does not need income, but is less tolerant of the volatility typical in aggressive growth funds. The resultant portfolio tempers higher growth potential with greater consistency of returns.

Figure 16

A Growth Portfolio

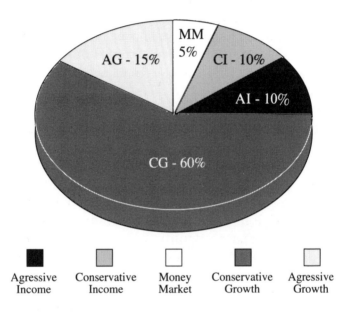

This is just one example of how a growth portfolio could be allocated.

As you can see, the assets allocated to growth funds in this growth portfolio drop to 75 percent. The growth allocation is further split between 15 percent aggressive growth and 60 percent conservative growth. Income funds are added to further reduce the portfolio's over-all risk and stabilize returns. The 20 percent income allocation is divided between 10 percent aggressive income and 10 percent conservative income. The remaining 5 percent is allocated to a money market fund.

This growth investor, too, could select 10 funds besides a money market fund. The aggressive growth portion of the portfolio could be filled with one aggressive growth/maximum capital appreciation fund, one small company growth fund and one specialty/sector fund. Three large company funds and two equity income funds could be selected for conservative growth. A high-yield municipal bond fund could be selected for aggressive income and an insured municipal bond fund for conservative income. Both of these municipal bond funds would contribute tax-free earnings for this investor, who may be in one of the higher tax brackets.

There are also investors who want to invest for growth, but prefer to hedge their growth even further with a greater allocation to income. Similar to the risk-reward tradeoff, there is a tradeoff between the amount of growth and income a portfolio can provide at any given time. If you structure your portfolio to provide you primarily with income, you will give up the opportunity for significant growth. If you structure your portfolio for growth, it can provide you with only so much in terms of consistent current income. If you attempt to improve either your growth potential or income, you will increase one at the expense of the other.

Figure 17 is one example of how assets could be allocated for a combined growth and income objective. This allocation creates more of a balance between the two asset categories. A balanced portfolio would provide greater growth potential than is available from a portfolio structured primarily for income, but it would not provide as much growth as a portfolio structured primarily for growth.

The investor who chooses to structure a portfolio for a combination of growth and income is actually more of a growth investor who would prefer to trade some growth potential for current income. Besides appreciating in capital, a balanced portfolio would grow through dividends and interest income, provided both are reinvested.

Figure 17

A Balanced Portfolio

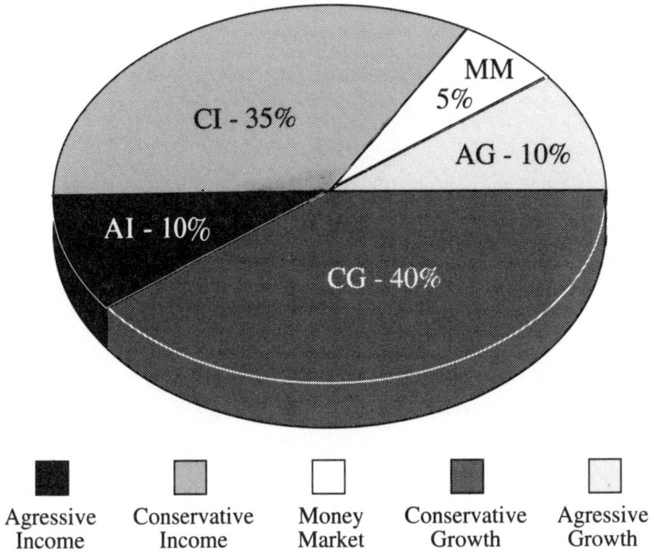

This is just one example of how a balanced portfolio could be allocated.

This balanced portfolio is made up of 50 percent growth and 45 percent income allocations. The aggressive growth allocation drops to 10 percent here and conservative growth represents 40 percent of the portfolio. The income allocation, however, increases to 45 percent and is split between 10 percent aggressive income and 35 percent conservative income. Five percent is put into a money market fund.

In addition to the money market fund, eight funds could suffice for this portfolio. An aggressive growth/maximum capital appreciation fund and a small company growth fund could be selected for aggressive growth. One large company growth fund, one equity income fund and one option income fund could be selected for conservative growth. For aggressive income this investor could choose a general corporate bond fund, which holds bonds of varying qualities. For conservative income, a high-quality corporate bond fund and a general government bond fund would be suitable.

If you are an investor who requires investment income in addition to what you receive from other sources, your investment objective will be primarily income-oriented. You will therefore want to allocate more of your assets to the income category. The remainder of your portfolio can be structured to provide you with some limited growth of capital. Figure 18 shows the shift in portfolio objective towards income.

Figure 18

An Income Portfolio

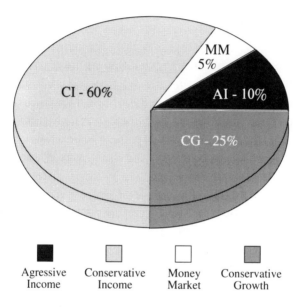

This is just one example of how an income portfolio
could be allocated.

Seventy percent of the assets in this portfolio are
allocated to income – 10 percent to aggressive income
and 60 percent to conservative income. Conservative
growth funds make up 25 percent of this portfolio. Once
again, 5 percent is allocated to a money market fund.

Why a 25 percent growth allocation for this income investor? There are two reasons, really. Not even income investors should automatically assume that bonds are the only choice for income. Income can also come from stock investments. Conservative growth funds, such as equity income funds, can provide some dividend income. Or, the capital gains earned through growth funds can be liquidated periodically for income. Although some income is possible from either of these stock funds, it is not as consistent as that earned from a bond fund.

Another reason for an income investor to invest for some growth is to overcome the effects of inflation. If you rely on your assets to produce income, you will need not only to preserve your asset base, you will also need to have your assets grow. Your assets can't grow to any great extent through interest-generating investments alone. So you should not allocate more assets to bond investments than are necessary to produce the required income. The remainder of your portfolio should be invested for growth.

In addition to the money market fund, this income portfolio could hold six funds. One large company growth fund, one equity income fund and one specialty/sector fund could be selected for conservative growth. A typical specialty fund in this instance might be a utility fund, used to produce income in addition to providing growth potential. One high-yield corporate bond fund could be used for aggressive income. And the selections for conservative income might include one U.S. Government bond fund and a high-quality corporate bond fund.

There are still other investors who must generate a higher level of income from their portfolios in order to meet living expenses. While they would be better off in attempting to pursue greater growth, they are more restricted in how they can structure their portfolios due to their income needs. Their need for income forces them to sacrifice a certain amount of growth.

Figure 19

A Maximum Income Portfolio

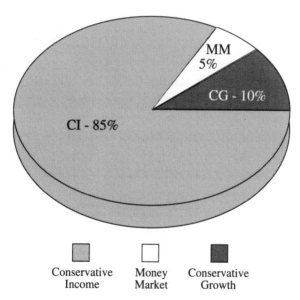

Conservative Income	Money Market	Conservative Growth

This is just one example of how a maximum income portfolio could be allocated.

Figure 19 shows how assets could be allocated for a maximum income portfolio. Almost the entire portfolio, 85 percent, is allocated for conservative income. What's left is split between 10 percent for conservative growth and 5 percent for a money market fund.

It isn't necessary to greatly diversify within the conservative income category because these funds typically have less market and credit risk. Thus, in addition to the money market fund, four funds could suffice for our maximum income investor. For the conservative growth portion of this portfolio, a growth and income fund might be suitable as it would provide a limited amount of income in addition to an opportunity for some growth. For conservative income, the selections could include a high-quality corporate bond fund and two U.S. Government bond funds that hold bonds with different average maturities.

As each of these sample portfolios illustrates, asset allocation is very personalized. Your portfolio is structured to be the most profitable for you, based on your current investment needs and risk parameters. Figure 20 shows that all investors begin at the same point. There are many mutual funds in the three different asset categories from which you may choose. As soon as you determine your investment objective, you begin to personalize your portfolio and narrow your possible fund choices. Your decision to invest for growth, income or growth and income will direct you to allocate your assets in the appropriate category.

Figure 20

Personalized Asset Allocation

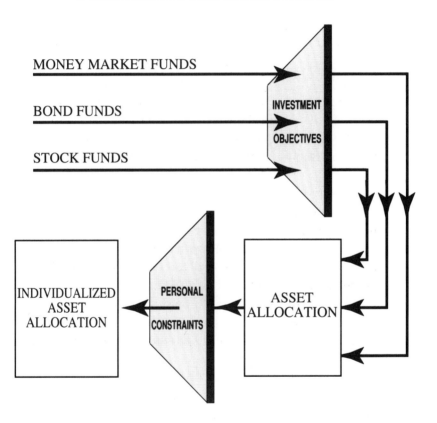

But it's at the point where you decide just how much risk you can assume that your portfolio begins to meet your personal needs. Two different investors may have a growth objective, for example, but one investor will be able to assume a higher level of risk than the other. While both investors would look at growth funds, the investor with a higher risk tolerance would allocate a greater proportion of assets to funds in the aggressive growth category, trading some consistency for the possibility of a higher long-term return. The investor with a lower risk tolerance would likely be more comfortable allocating a greater proportion of assets to conservative growth funds, since they tend to offset lower returns with less volatility.

A similar scenario could arise with income investors. Although both need income, the investor with lower risk tolerance would structure a portfolio toward conservative income, relying more on government bond funds with shorter maturities. The aggressive income investor could consider allocating more dollars to corporate bond funds, perhaps with longer maturities. The corporate bond funds would likely provide a slightly higher long-term return at a greater risk.

To reiterate, you need to determine what you want your portfolio to accomplish. Only you know how much income you require, how much of your portfolio you can allocate to growth, and how much risk you can tolerate. That's what will differentiate your portfolio from another investor's. If your investment objective or your risk tolerance changes, it should be reflected in your asset allocation and your resultant fund selections.

MUTUAL FUND SELECTION

You've come to the third and final step in Diversified Mutual Fund Investing – mutual fund selection. This is the step in which you will actually select funds by analyzing fund performance and the variables that can impact a fund's performance. Following the Diversified Mutual Fund Investing methodology will enable you to confidently select a group of funds most suitable for your portfolio based on your investment objective and risk-adjusted fund returns.

The number of funds you should select for your portfolio will depend on the amount of money you wish to invest and your overall diversification needs. Five funds may be enough for one investor, while another may require 10 or even 15 funds to be sufficiently diversified. It is unnecessary to spread your money over too many funds; beyond a certain number of funds, there is no further advantage to you in diversifying.

As Figure 21 shows, your selections may be made from the aggressive growth, conservative growth, aggressive income, conservative income, or money market fund categories. Once again, the actual number of funds you select will depend upon the amount of money you have to invest and the number of selections you will need to be sufficiently diversified. There is a greater need to diversify among funds within the aggressive growth or aggressive income categories as aggressive funds have higher risk. You do not need to diversify to the same extent within the conservative growth or conservative income categories because there is less risk with conservative funds. As for your liquidity, one good quality money market fund should be sufficient.

Figure 21

Diversified Mutual Fund Investing

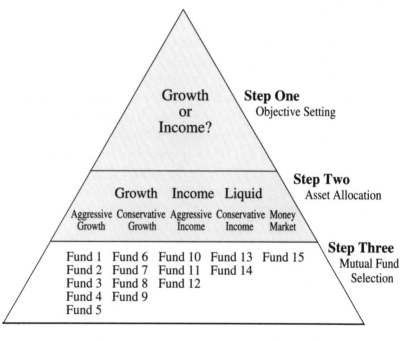

The number of funds in each category is for illustrative purposes only.

ANALYZING FUND PERFORMANCE

Ideally you'll want to begin your fund analysis by focusing on all of the funds in the category that will best meet your investment objective. If your primary objective is growth, you should start by looking at growth funds, both aggressive and conservative. If your primary objective is income, you should begin by looking at income funds. Then, based on your risk constraints, you can further narrow your choices.

Before you can select the best risk-adjusted performers for your portfolio, you will need to weigh a fund's level of return and its level of risk. You will be looking at how well each fund has performed relative to the other funds in the group and considering the fund's return relative to the risks the fund has taken. As part of your fund analysis, you will also need to assess the factors described in the previous chapter.

Comparing Fund Returns

Although there are a number of elements you should pay attention to during your analysis, the greatest emphasis should be placed on those factors that directly relate to fund performance. The most visible indicator of fund performance is total return. You should begin your fund performance comparison by looking at the annual total returns of the funds you are considering. A fund's total return numbers include dividends as well as any capital gains or losses.

Before you can make a sound judgment about a fund's suitability for your portfolio, you will want to examine a fund's past as well as present performance. Many investors tend to overlook the fact that the latest fund returns will tell them little about a fund. To assess true investment potential you need to look at a fund's historical returns for as long a period as possible.

How consistently has the fund performed over time? Successful mutual fund investing means investing in funds that consistently perform well on a risk-adjusted basis. In the same way that the past year's fund performance provides you with little information about a fund, the past year's performance gives you little indication of a fund's consistency of returns. You should be looking for strong performance over an extended time period and in both up and down markets.

Even though there is no way to accurately predict fund performance, you can use a fund's performance history to make some assumptions about a fund's potential and the probability that it will continue to achieve a certain level of performance. Although there are no guarantees, funds with a long and consistently successful performance history are more likely to perform well in the future.

But just how can you compare funds? How can you determine whether one fund is better than another? One way is to see how well each fund has performed in relation to the market each year. To do so, you'll need to compare a fund's year-to-year returns to certain performance benchmarks. Stock fund returns can be compared to an index of overall stock market performance, an example of which is the Standard & Poor's 500. Bond fund returns can be measured against the Lehman Brothers Bond Index.

A better way to compare fund performance is by "averaging" each fund's annual returns. You can then use average annual return as a measure of one fund's performance relative to other funds in the group. To determine a fund's average annual return, you first add together the annual return percentages for each of the years. Then divide the total by the number of years covered in your calculation. This will give you the average annual return. You can calculate the average annual return in the same manner for any fund in your comparison group and you can use these averages to rank the funds relative to each other.

Morningstar's fund rating system assesses fund performance beginning with calculating average returns. Annual total returns are ranked on a percentile scale from one to 100 in this system, enabling you, if you wish, to compare one fund's annual return to other funds and to funds with the same objective. In this purely "total return ranking," smaller numbers signify better returns. Funds with total returns that rank in the top 25 percent or bottom 25 percent tend to be riskier, while funds in the middle range tend to produce steadier long-term returns.

Morningstar's fund return rating, however, is not based solely on a fund's annual returns. The return rating places an even greater emphasis on historical performance. A fund's returns are weighted differently for various time periods, with more recent fund returns considered least indicative of future fund performance. The heaviest weighting is placed on a fund's 10-year performance; the average annual return for the last 10 years is given a 50 percent weighting. The average annual return for the past five years is weighted at 30 percent. And the return for the last three years gets only a 20 percent weighting. If a fund has been in operation for only five years, the five-year return is given a 60 percent weighting and three-year performance is weighted at 40 percent. This is the calculation used as the basis of a fund's return rating. Any detrimental effect of loads and other fees on fund returns is also considered before a fund's performance is rated.

What differentiates this system from others is that the risk aspect of fund performance is considered in addition to returns. Fund ratings include calculations of both load-adjusted return and risk, which provide you with a more complete assessment of fund performance. This system can help you identify funds which produce high levels of returns and those that take high risks, allowing you to make your selections accordingly.

Adjusting Return For Risk

Every investor would like to outperform the market. But not everyone would be comfortable with even matching the market's performance. Why? Because of the market's volatility. Remember that if you buy shares in a fund that duplicates the market, you will match the market's returns and the market's volatility.

Thus, a fund's returns are only one aspect of fund selection. The other is return volatility, or risk. Risk is apparent in the fluctuating market value of a fund and is reflected in the up-and-down movement of a fund's price per share.

If you're considering a fund with superior performance, you need to look at how that fund's returns were achieved. Exceptional performance can mean little if a fund's returns are volatile. Investing in a fund that performs well above the market when the market is moving up could mean a plummet just as far in the other direction when the market takes a downturn. Investing in a fund that underperforms the market can mean lower returns, but it may also mean less volatility.

The goal of Diversified Mutual Fund Investing is to find mutual funds with the best risk-adjusted performance, meaning they produce the highest levels of returns possible relative to their level of risk. Looking at it another way, you should seek funds with returns that show less volatility relative to a given level of performance. If three funds have similar returns, for example, it would make the most sense to select the fund with returns that are the most consistent. It is also more profitable to seek funds that will perform well over an extended period without excessive volatility.

Many funds can produce high returns over a short period of time, but achieving consistent performance over extended time periods is more difficult. Risk-adjusted mutual fund investing will protect your money during times when the market is performing poorly; during downward market movements, good risk-adjusted funds will be less subject to market volatility than other funds in your comparison group.

Another part of your fund analysis, then, is to weigh the risk level against the level of returns for each fund in your comparison group. One way to assess fund risk is to compare year-to-year fund performance, which will provide you with some indication of a fund's volatility. A fund that has performed consistently is more likely to continue to perform consistently.

In addition, mutual funds can be rated for risk the same way individual securities are rated. Although beta measures were developed to rate individual stocks, they can be applied to mutual funds as well. As with stocks, the market, once again, has a beta value of 1.00, representing average volatility. A fund with a beta value of 2.00 would display twice as much volatility as the market. A fund with a beta value of less than 1.00 would fluctuate less than the market. A fund's beta value can change as internal fund variables change. You can obtain a fund's beta value by calling the fund, or through a number of financial publications.

Morningstar's system rates funds for risk based on a comparison of fund performance to T-bill returns. T-bills, of course, have no volatility and always provide a positive return.

Unlike the more typical measures of risk, which take into account both positive and negative fund deviation, this system focuses only on negative deviation.

Monthly fund returns that are lower than 90-day T-bill rates are considered negative and the fund producing them would receive a lower rating. Fund performance lower than T-bills would also indicate greater fund volatility.

To calculate a fund's risk, the 90-day T-bill rate is subtracted from each month's fund returns. The amounts by which a fund's returns trail T-bill returns are added together. The total is then divided by the number of months in the rating period. This number is compared to the numbers from other funds. Each fund is then assigned a risk ranking. The 10 percent of the funds with the largest monthly losses are considered to have the highest risk, the next group is considered to have above-average risk, then average risk, below-average risk and low risk. Yearly risk totals are then weighted in the same way as fund returns, with a 50 percent emphasis placed on 10-year risk, followed by a 30 percent weighting for five-year risk and a 20 percent weighting for three-year risk.

As with total return, funds are also ranked for risk on a percentile scale. They are ranked for risk in comparison to all funds, and to funds with the same objective. In this case, also, a lower score is a better score; a lower score would indicate a fund with lower risk.

Combining Return And Risk Factors

This system attempts to aid investors in selecting funds that provide consistently strong returns. Highly-rated funds are the ones that investors will be most likely to hold long enough to reap profits. Assigning higher ratings to consistent performers also encourages investors to take a long-term approach to mutual fund investing and avoid the trap of buying high and selling low. Buying high-risk funds at price peaks can mean waiting years just to break even. Worse yet, when you buy high you may be tempted to sell out at a time when the fund's returns hit a low point.

The highest ratings are given to funds that produce high returns with relatively low risk or volatility. Based on this system, funds with low returns and low risk or high returns with high risk are considered average performers because you would tend to expect low returns in compensation for low risk and high returns in compensation for high risk. It is also assumed the returns from high-risk funds would have to be very high to adequately compensate investors, and few investors would be willing to tolerate a level of risk high enough to earn such an offsetting gain.

Return and risk scores are adjusted so that 1.00 equals the average return or risk for funds in the comparison group, as with beta measures. Scores above or below 1.00 would indicate a fund with return or risk above or below the group's average. For example, a fund with a return rating of 1.25 would indicate a fund that produces a return 25 percent above average when compared to other funds in the group. A risk rating of 0.75 would indicate a fund that has 25 percent less risk than other funds in the group.

After a fund's return and risk ratings are calculated

separately, they are combined with equal weighting for a final fund performance ranking. These final rankings show how the fund performed in relation to all funds and to funds with the same objective. Stock funds, taxable bond funds and municipal bond funds are also rated separately. Hybrid funds (funds that do not fit solely in either the growth or income category) are rated against all funds except municipal bond funds.

Although this system considers risk and return equally in its final fund ratings, it is set up so that you may consider each portion of the rating individually if you wish. While it is not recommended that you select a high-performance, high-risk fund since there are so many lower-risk, high-performance funds available, you may choose to place greater emphasis on the return portion of the fund rating. If, on the other hand, security is more important, you may place greater emphasis on the risk portion of the rating to help you select funds with the least volatility.

A fund's rating in this system can change if the performance of other funds within the comparison group changes. Although a particular fund may continue to perform well, if the performance of other funds in the group improves, the fund's ranking will fall relative to the other funds. This kind of change does not necessarily mean you should sell your holdings in the fund, but you may want to consider your alternative choices within the fund group at that time.

Once you review the level of returns and relative risk of each fund you are considering, and look at any other factors that can influence fund performance, it becomes much easier to make informed choices. While there may be other methods available to compare funds, this system of separately evaluating fund return and risk is one of the most logical methods you can use to decide which funds would be most appropriate for your portfolio. You need to know the risks connected with a fund's returns before you can confidently select funds that are the best risk-adjusted performers and before you can build a Diversified Mutual Fund portfolio that will help you reach your investment objective.

MONITORING YOUR PORTFOLIO

As a Diversified Mutual Fund investor, you want a portfolio that will continue to produce consistent results. You should attempt to maintain holdings of the best risk-adjusted funds available to you. While there will be times when it will be in your best interest to sell some of your holdings, maintaining a portfolio of funds does not mean constantly buying and selling fund shares. Nevertheless, you will need to put some effort into making certain the funds in your portfolio are consistently achieving the highest risk-adjusted returns possible.

Many investors use the mutual fund listings found in the newspaper. While you can look in the newspaper to find out how your funds are performing on a daily basis, such frequent checking is not really necessary if you have selected your funds properly. The listings will give you yesterday's net asset value of your funds, but any very short-term fluctuations mean little.

The funds that you invest in will send you statements of the activity in your account. You will also receive monthly, quarterly or annual reports from the funds. You can use this information to help you keep track of how well your funds are performing. You can compare the reports and look for any significant changes that could indicate a problem.

You should not necessarily sell your fund holdings if the net asset value drops; a fund's net asset value will likely decline after dividends or capital gains are distributed, or in conjunction with periodic corrections in the stock or bond market. You do not need to sell your holdings when a fund becomes overvalued — which is to say when it reaches a selling point — because such a concept does not apply to mutual funds specifically. In other words, you should make certain you are not selling your fund shares hastily as even the best funds don't necessarily display outstanding performance every quarter.

You could hire a professional asset manager to relieve you of the need to keep track of your portfolio's progress. This would be someone able to actively manage your fund investments and make changes in your portfolio's composition as needed. An asset manager can make certain that you are receiving the highest returns possible. For providing this service, an asset manager receives a management fee which is a percentage of the money you have invested.

While fund reports will tell you the status of your funds, you need to keep track of how well they are performing in relation to the other funds in the same category – the funds you could have chosen instead. To do so you will need to work through the Diversified Mutual Fund Investing process over and over again to determine whether your funds are still the best selections available to you. Always keep your investment objective in mind when you compare your ideal position to where you are currently. A fund is only a best choice if it meets your investment objective and your risk constraints. And your focus can only be on whether a given fund is appropriate for you at present.

So how do you decide when you should sell your funds? There are several situations which could cause you to reconsider your holdings. The first would be a change in your investment objective. While a fund's objective can remain constant for years, your own objective and financial needs may change. The composition of your portfolio should then be adjusted to meet your evolving needs. Or your investment emphasis may shift slightly; you may decide to place a greater emphasis on either reducing your risk or increasing your returns.

Another reason to reconsider your fund holdings is a determination that your investment objective can be better met by another fund. Such a possibility can become obvious once you again work through the Diversified Mutual Fund Investing process. Perhaps you overlooked other strong, risk-adjusted performers. Or, changes might have occurred within a fund itself. A fund's objective, manager or investment strategy can change. You should question your holdings if any of these developments occurs.

And no matter how carefully you selected your funds as part of Diversified Mutual Fund Investing, a fund may just not be performing as it should be. Or, different funds within the same fund group may simply be performing much better. If such a situation should occur and you are convinced that your fund is no longer among the best performers in your portfolio, it's probably time to sell your holdings and reinvest in funds with better performance.

Just as there is no such thing as a risk-free investment, neither is there such a thing as a permanent investment. You can't expect to invest your money and then totally forget about it. You can begin with funds that match your objective, that are good risk-adjusted performers and have sound management. But there will likely come a time when you will have to reconsider your holdings. The best way to gauge whether you should sell your shares is to stay aware of how well your funds are measuring up to other funds in the same category on a risk-adjusted basis. Only then can you decide whether they are still the most appropriate choices for your portfolio.

Chapter 5

Mutual Fund Implementation Strategies

You've determined your investment objective. You've allocated your assets between stock, bond and money market funds to meet your investment objective. And you've selected funds for your portfolio that have the best risk-adjusted performance. Now that you've worked through the Diversified Mutual Fund Investing process, you still face the task of purchasing fund shares.

Just how should you go about making your fund purchases? Should you invest your money in one lump sum, or move into the market gradually over a period of time? Are there any better times to buy or sell fund shares? Should you watch the market?

Although you can simply mail checks to the funds you have selected, doing so is not necessarily the most profitable way to move your money into the market. You've already taken the time to structure your portfolio. You've made the effort to thoroughly analyze your alternatives before selecting appropriate funds. Why not try to purchase your fund shares when it would be more advantageous for you to do so?

Just as there are strategies for selecting mutual funds, there are strategies you can use to buy or sell fund shares on a more opportunistic basis. Following these strategies does not require that you keep track of every market movement and attempt to time your fund purchases and sales. Market timing, as you will see, is a strategy that does not work as well as its proponents would lead you to believe. Dollar cost averaging, on the other hand, is a smart way to buy or sell fund shares.

Yet there are broad and statistically significant market trends that you can use to your advantage if you are aware of them. Without timing the market, you will see that there are more opportune times to buy or sell shares based on extremes in the market and consumer sentiment. According to historical data, there are also better times of the year, better months of the year and better days of the week to buy or sell shares.

So if you are planning to move your money into the market, why not use some of these strategies to your benefit? If you're going to buy shares of funds that will meet your investment objective, anyway, you may find these fund implementation strategies to be of some assistance.

TIMING THE MARKET

One investment strategy long used in the stock market is market timing, or attempting to shift money in synch with market movements. The goal of market timers is to move money into the market just before it moves up to catch the upward movement and maximize gains, and then pull out just before a downslide to avoid losses.

Market timers follow economic, political and monetary trends to help them determine the most opportune moments for buying or selling. They want to be in stocks when the time is right, and out when it's not. They want to be in bonds when bonds are the highest performing category. And they want to be in cash when that's the best place to have their money.

Knowing the best times to be in or out of the market is every investor's dream. In theory, timing helps you achieve high profits and reduce risk. In practice, however, timing the market is not quite so simple. A perfect market timer who invested $1 in 1926, with interest compounded, would have had $2,650,000 in 1988. Or, $1 million invested in 1926 would have grown to $2.65 trillion by 1988, more than all of the market shares of all the publicly traded companies in North America. That didn't happen.

Studies have shown that to outperform the market long-term, timers need to be correct 70 percent of the time in their predictions. How likely are they to achieve such an average? About 62 percent of the time the market goes up, and 38 percent of the time it goes down, according to data by Ibbotson and Sinquefield.

If an up market occurs 62 percent of the time and timers are able to correctly predict such a market 70 percent of the time, there is a 43 percent probability overall that they will correctly predict an up market. If a down market occurs 38 percent of the time and timers are able to predict that occurrence 70 percent of the time, they would have a 27 percent probability of predicting down markets and being out of the market at the right time. Those are not exactly the best odds.

According to research, to invest profitably it's more important to be in the market during the upswings than out of the market during downslides, because a disproportionate amount of the gain is made off the bottom of the cycle, just as the market begins to move up. One 1984 study showed that if you missed the three best quarters from 1975 to 1982, you would have achieved only average returns! Another study showed that if you're going to achieve above-average returns and you're 100 percent accurate in predicting up markets, you need to be less than one percent accurate in predicting down markets. This 100 percent accuracy translates to a buy-and-hold strategy, meaning if you simply get into the market and stay there, you will statistically do as well as a market timer who predicts up markets accurately only 70 percent of the time. It was also found that a market timer who is less than 60 percent accurate in predicting up markets will actually underperform the buy-and-hold strategy.

Professional market timers do not have a very good record of trying to predict what will happen in the market. Money management companies that practice market timing have not been able to achieve solid or consistent results. Although the economy follows cyclical patterns, it's very difficult to predict the exact duration or direction of each market movement with great accuracy. Today's market shifts more abruptly and unpredictably than it did in the past.

Some market timers advise switching between stock, bond and money market funds based on economic indicators. Funds that allow you to switch in and out may charge a nominal $5 or $10 fee. Some funds will charge you a penalty for moving your money out within a very short time after you have invested because switching between funds often disrupts a fund manager's investment portfolio. Regardless, you still face the same risks in trying to time mutual funds as you do with individual stocks and bonds; you take the chance of buying and selling at the wrong times.

It's been said that if you can predict the economy, you can predict the market. But few, if any analysts can predict the economy. What's most important is that you select strong performing funds in asset categories that will meet your investment objective for growth, income or liquidity. Selecting funds according to the category that is most likely to perform the best at a given point in time is unlikely to help you reach your investment goal.

DOLLAR COST AVERAGING

Since we can't accurately predict when a fund's price per share will be the lowest, it is important that you move your money into the market gradually. This practice, known as "dollar cost averaging," is one of the most efficient ways to purchase mutual fund shares. Using this strategy to buy fund shares at different prices over time, you will "average out" the cost; your investment dollars will buy fewer shares when the share price is higher and more shares when the price is lower. Following this strategy is one way you can reduce your chances of buying all of your fund shares when the price per share is at a peak.

Figure 22 shows that if, for example, you chose to buy fund shares in $1,000 monthly allotments over the course of a year, sometimes you would have bought shares when the price was a bit lower and sometimes when it was a bit higher. But, overall, the purchase price would have averaged out to less than the highest price; your fund purchases would have averaged $12.84 per share instead of the $13.22 high.

Figure 22

Dollar Cost Averaging

Investment	Price Per Share	Shares Purchased
$1,000	$12.49	80.06
$1,000	$12.67	78.92
$1,000	$12.85	77.82
$1,000	$13.05	76.62
$1,000	$12.92	77.39
$1,000	$12.80	78.12
$1,000	$12.73	78.55
$1,000	$12.66	78.98
$1,000	$12.78	78.24
$1,000	$12.91	77.45
$1,000	$13.10	76.33
$1,000	$13.22	75.64
$12,000 total	$12.84 average	934.12 total

It's important that you invest money regularly, be it weekly, monthly or quarterly. You want to buy shares consistently over time to improve your chances of purchasing shares at a lower average price. The more volatile the fund you're investing in, the longer the period of time over which you should be dollar cost averaging. This strategy saves you from trying to predict the market each time you move in and still allows you to accumulate shares cost-effectively.

But what happens if you select what turns out to be the worst possible times to average into a fund? What if you pick the days when the fund's price per share is at its peak? You will probably still make money!

Figure 23 shows the results of investing $5,000 every year for 15 years on the day when The Growth Fund of America's price per share was highest.

Figure 23

Investing in the
Growth Fund of America

Date of Market High	Cumulative Investment	Account Value at Year's End
9/21/76	$ 5,000	$ 4,915
1/3/77	$10,000	$ 11,532
9/8/78	$15,000	$ 18,687
10/5/79	$20,000	$ 32,324
11/20/80	$25,000	$ 49,914
4/27/81	$30,000	$ 54,664
12/27/82	$35,000	$ 73,291
11/29/83	$40,000	$ 97,702
1/ 6/84	$45,000	$ 96,710
12/16/85	$50,000	$127,688
12/ 2/86	$55,000	$153,035
8/25/87	$60,000	$168,017
10/21/88	$65,000	$203,878
10/ 9/89	$70,000	$269,774
7/16/90	$75,000	$262,934

Assuming you had reinvested all dividends and capital gains, your $75,000 investment would have grown to $262,934 for an average annual compound return of 15.5 percent. Not bad for selecting the worst day to invest every year, for 15 years straight. Granted, if you had selected the best day each year to invest that $5,000, your account would have been worth $318,021 at the end of 1990. But had you simply kept the $75,000 in a savings account earning 5.25 percent compounded annually over that same time period, your account would have been valued at no more than $161,582.

Another buying strategy you may want to consider is not to purchase fund shares just before a fund pays out a dividend or capital gain. If you do, you may receive a realized capital gain that you did not actually earn and you will have to pay tax on what is, in effect, a return of your principal. The remainder of your investment will be worth less because once the dividend is paid, the fund's share price may also drop. For example, if you invest $10,000 November 15 and a dividend and capital gains payment is made November 30, you are paid $2,000 or 20 percent on your invested after-tax dollars. The $2,000 is considered income that you have to pay taxes on even though you didn't earn it.

Just as you cannot predict the best times to buy fund shares, you cannot predict the best times to sell your shares, either. As with purchasing fund shares, dollar cost averaging is one of the best strategies to use in liquidating your holdings. Utilizing this strategy will make it more likely that you won't sell all of your shares at the lowest point.

Or if the shares you hold are in a fund family that includes a money market fund, you could liquidate your shares by first moving your money into the money market fund; in this way you will receive the day's closing share price. Then you can proceed to mail your letter to the fund to receive your liquidation without being concerned that the price per share will drop in the meantime.

Another strategy to consider is not to sell your fund shares just before dividends or capital gains are distributed, as you won't receive them. To receive such a distribution, you must be a shareholder of record on a particular date.

HISTORICAL MARKET TENDENCIES

Statistics show that there are general tendencies of the market to be up or down at certain points in time. These market trends would indicate that there are actually better times to buy or sell shares in the market. While there is no way to accurately predict when the market will be up or down, if you must buy or sell fund shares anyway, you may find these tendencies of the market to be of some limited value. Making use of these strategies is not the same as market timing; you will not need to watch daily market swings or interest rate movements. Using these strategies also will not guarantee that you will outperform the market. These are simply historical tendencies that you can use to possibly stretch your investment dollars at the time you are planning on buying or selling fund shares.

EXTREMES IN MARKET SENTIMENT

Most of us believe we are aware of the overall state of the U.S. economy at any given time. We're in the midst of talk about the national budget, the business climate, the market and global politics. We read newspaper articles and hear television and radio reports. The state of the economy is also apparent in our daily lives. We know when unemployment is up or down. And, if nothing else, we are consumers; we can see what happens to prices in stores and we notice whether or not people are spending money.

When everyone feels everything is going pretty well, economic sentiment is positive and consumers are more willing to buy. During recessionary periods the mood is more somber and consumers tend to hold on to their dollars longer. This consumer sentiment about the economy is an emotional attitude that also affects the market. How consumers "feel" about the state of things will determine not only whether they spend, but whether they will invest. When the general economic climate is very optimistic, people tend to invest and cash reserves are low. When the climate is pessimistic, people tend to sell and cash reserves climb higher. Unfortunately, those who follow the general sentiment of the crowd at extremes of the market are doing exactly the opposite of what they should be doing. It is at the very top and bottom of this economic cycle that people tend to miss some of the best buying and selling opportunities.

When the economy is in a severe recession and the business climate is bad, investors take losses and anticipate further bad news. When the market hits bottom, investors usually sell their holdings because they expect economic hard times to continue. Yet it's at this point that the upswing tends to begin. Many people don't realize that the Federal Reserve usually starts to loosen credit as the economy slows. Interest rates then begin to fall, and stocks become more attractive as the return on cash drops. Typically the economy will remain on the downside for several more months, but it's at this pessimistic market extreme that a perceptive investor would most likely go against the crowd and buy. A down market is typically near its end when the crowd continues to be extremely pessimistic during the first sharp market upswing. The crowd regards the upswing as a time to sell instead of a time to buy.

The problem is that it's difficult for investors to be optimistic about investing during economic downturns. As interest rates start to decline, market activity is generated. This renewed buying activity initiates the market rally and pushes stock prices up. But investors waiting for an opportune time to buy tend not to believe a new market rally has begun, although it is typically the strongest rally in the cycle. And the next market decline never seems to be large enough to make the majority of investors comfortable about jumping in.

When prices drop slightly, some investors will start to buy back into the market; the decline ends and other investors miss the chance to buy in at lower prices. The trend continues as the market inches higher and higher. More and more people move into the market and it becomes saturated. Near the top of the up market, people are extremely optimistic. There are brief sell-offs and the market bounces back quickly, rising to higher levels. But the crowd anticipates that the market will reach even higher levels. This peak is another instance of a market extreme and is the right time to sell before a major correction takes place.

By the time the market reaches such a high point, most of the cash reserves are used up and the market can only maintain itself. There is great speculation, stocks carry high price/earnings ratios and there is little liquidity. A small rise in interest rates can easily trigger a market downturn. On the first true market decline, people rush out to invest, anticipating even higher prices. But this first rally fails, the decline hits, and prices drop even further. Although investors begin to get nervous and start selling, it takes many sell-offs over many months before pessimism takes hold, business conditions worsen and the down market hits bottom.

In the same way that investors make the mistake of chasing a top fund and catching it just before a big drop, many investors stop investing when the market declines. Typically they don't start investing again until the market is higher. They move into the market long after a rally has been underway and sell after the worst part of a decline is over. Instead, they should be doing just the opposite. It's at the extremes of the cycle that the best buying and selling opportunities tend to occur.

The point is to be aware of extremes in either market optimism or pessimism. While it may be difficult to clearly discern extremes in the market except in hindsight, it is when the market is extremely one-sided that you would want to go against the crowd, if possible. Market extremes will vary from cycle to cycle, yet measures of consumer sentiment will give you a rough idea of the degree of optimism or pessimism prevalent. When the crowd becomes extreme it is, if nothing else, a time for caution.

FUND CASH-TO-ASSET RATIOS

The overall condition of the market and consumer sentiment will also be reflected in mutual funds. Fund cash flow is largely controlled by the actions of shareholders. When shareholders invest, there is more money available in the fund for fund managers to invest. When shareholders want to redeem their shares, fund managers must respond by selling fund holdings and moving to cash. Thus, the amount of cash in a fund will indicate the general sentiment of shareholders and the market.

More specifically, you can determine how optimistic or pessimistic shareholders are by looking at a fund's cash-to-asset ratio. This ratio is calculated by dividing the fund's cash by its assets. When shareholders are optimistic, they pump more money into funds. Fund managers, seeing a larger amount of cash coming in, will invest more heavily for the fund, causing the cash-to-asset ratio to fall. If, however, shareholders are pessimistic about the market and fund managers anticipate shareholder redemptions, they will sell fund holdings and allow the amount of cash in the fund to increase, causing the cash-to-asset ratio to rise.

Extremes in fund cash-to-asset ratios indicate extremes in market sentiment. Extreme lows in fund cash-to-asset ratios indicate extreme market optimism; extreme highs in the ratios indicate extreme market pessimism. Such extremes in fund cash-to-asset ratios are one more tendency you may wish to consider when you are buying or selling shares. As with extremes of crowd sentiment, it's not always so easy to determine exactly when funds hit extreme highs or lows in cash-to-asset ratios except in hindsight.

The fund market indication record in Figure 24 shows the extremes of fund optimism and pessimism as reflected in the extreme lows and highs of the funds' cash-to-asset ratios from 1956 to 1988. Figure 24 is based on a chart constructed by Martin Zweig using information obtained from The Investment Company Institute in Washington, D.C.

Figure 24

Fund Market Indication Record
1956-1988

Date	Cash/Asset Ratio Low (optimistic)	Cash/Asset Ratio High (pessimistic)	DOW*	DOW's Change Before Next Fund Extreme	Fund Market Indications Right	Fund Market Indications Wrong
7/56	4.7%		516	− 29		X
6/58		7.2%	487	+ 148		X
4/59	4.4%		635	− 57		X
9/60		6.6%	578	+ 123		X
12/61	4.3%		701	− 128		X
9/62		7.0%	573	+ 296		X
11/64	4.5%		869	− 60		X
10/66		9.7%	809	+ 88		X
9/67	5.2%		897	+ 1	X	
3/68		9.2%	898	+ 38		X
12/68	6.1%		936	− 191		X
7/70		11.8%	745	+ 217		X
4/72	4.6%		962	− 307		X
9/74		13.5%	655	+ 282		X
9/76	4.9%		937	− 124		X
3/78		11.3%	813	+ 25		X
9/78	6.9%		838	+ 32	X	
5/80		10.4%	870	+ 136		X
3/81	8.0%		1006	− 177		X
6/82		11.7%	829	+ 430		X
12/83	7.5%		1259	− 158		X
6/84		10.3%	1101	+ 166		X
3/85	8.1%		1267	+ 168	X	
10/85		10.4%	1435	+ 334		X
2/86	8.4%		1769	+ 68	X	
9/86		10.2%	1837	+ 439		X
3/87	8.6%		2276	− 323		X
4/88		10.9%	1953	+ 198		X
11/88			2151			

*Dow price is third Friday of the following month, when cash to assets data are made available to the public.

Looking at Figure 24 you can see that in July 1956, for example, the cash-to-asset ratio for mutual funds hit a low of 4.7 percent. At the time, the DOW was at 516. On the surface, such extreme optimism suggested the market was headed up. But look at what had happened to the DOW by the time the funds' cash-to-asset ratio hit the next extreme – it had dropped 29 points to 487, despite the prevailing optimism. The funds' indication of the market's direction was wrong; instead of rising, the market fell. In reality, this extreme of optimism meant the funds were heavily invested. It was consumer sentiment that was swaying fund investment levels. Investors poured money into funds when they were optimistic and the funds in turn used up much of their cash reserves to invest in the market. Once these cash reserves had been depleted, there was little or no room for the market to expand. The next major market movement had to be down. And so it was, with the DOW dropping 29 points.

As with extremes in market sentiment, extremes in fund cash-to-asset ratios indicate instances when you may be better off going against the crowd. Extreme fund optimism would be a better selling than buying opportunity. Market prices tend to peak at these moments of optimism. Funds will run out of cash reserves and the climbing market will lose steam. When everyone is extremely optimistic, you need to brace yourself for a drop.

Now look at what happened in June 1958 in Figure 24. The funds' cash-to-asset ratio hit 7.2 percent, an extreme of pessimism. The DOW was at 487 points.

Again, on the surface you would think this pessimistic point would indicate an impending downturn of the market. But at the next extreme in the funds' cash-to-asset ratio the DOW moved in the opposite direction, up 148 points. The majority was wrong again and the funds' cash-to-asset ratio reflected the error by hitting an extreme cash high. This time, as the shareholders sensed a continuing decline, they cashed in shares and forced the funds to take larger cash positions.

Just as with extremes of market pessimism, extremes of fund pessimism may present good buying opportunities. It is at these points that fund share prices tend to be lowest. The next market extreme is likely to be a high point, as shown by the historical data. You may not always be in a position to consider market extremes, but if you are able to take advantage of them, you may be able to get more for your investment dollars.

FUND ADVISORY SERVICES

Many investors trust fund advisory services for opinions on the best times to invest. But even if you don't, the sentiment of advisors is another indication of the general outlook of the market. Figure 25 on the next page shows the record of investment advisory services from 1965 to 1988. This chart, constructed by Martin Zweig, is based on information from Investors' Intelligence of Larchmont, New York.

Figure 25

Advisory Services Record 1965-1988

Date	% of Advisors Bullish			Dow's Change Before Next Advisory Extreme	Advisory Market Predictions	
	Extreme Optimism	Extreme Pessimism	Dow		Right	Wrong
4/23/65	89.7%		911	− 48		X
7/30/65		41.4%	863	+ 125		X
1/26/66	90.9%		988	− 217		X
10/19/66		28.0%	771	+ 159		X
9/20/67	70.6%		930	− 90		X
4/3/67		13.7%	840	+ 74		X
6/12/68	69.8%		914	− 18		X
9/4/68		31.6%	896	+ 70		X
12/25/68	68.8%		966	− 62		X
3/21/69		25.7%	904	+ 57		X
5/16/69	61.0%		961	− 143		X
8/1/69		19.6%	818	+ 42		X
11/14/69	63.1%		860	− 142		X
5/15/70		31.2%	718	+ 195		X
3/26/71	85.0%		913	− 55		X
8/6/71		50.0%	858	+ 55		X
9/10/71	82.1%		913	− 96		X
11/26/71		50.0%	817	+ 210		X
12/15/72	85.0%		1027	− 107		X
6/ 8/73		38.8%	920	+ 59		X
10/12/73	69.4%		979	− 157		X
11/30/73		35.9%	822	+ 56		X
3/22/74	64.4%		878	− 191		X
8/23/74		29.1%	687	+ 63		X
2/21/75	79.1%		750	+ 76	X	
8/15/75		46.4%	826	+ 146		X

Figure 25 (continued)

Date	% of Advisors Bullish		Dow	Dow's Change Before Next Advisory Extreme	Advisory Market Predictions	
	Extreme Optimism	Extreme Pessimism			Right	Wrong
1/14/77	94.6%		972	− 196		X
2/10/78		27.6%	776	+ 121		X
8/13/78	79.7%		897	− 74		X
11/ 3/78		29.2%	823	+ 57		X
8/24/79	60.3%		880	− 74		X
11/ 9/79		22.1%	806	+ 75		X
2/1/80	62.1%		881	− 69		X
3/14/80		27.1%	812	+ 128		X
9/26/80	67.6%		940	− 4		X
2/20/81		35.9%	936	+ 71		X
4/ 3/81	61.0%		1007	− 171		· X
9/18/81		28.7%	836	+ 20		X
11/13/81	59.7%		856	− 51		X
6/ 4/82		27.0%	805	+ 437		X
6/24/83	82.9%		1242	− 118		X
6/1/84		36.6%	1124	+ 175		X
3/1/85	82.0%		1299	+ 30	X	
10/4/85		47.7%	1329	+ 410		X
4/4/86	86.6%		1739	+ 31	X	
9/26/86		46.8%	1770	+ 454		X
2/27/87	83.1%		2224	− 230		X
10/30/87		37.2%	1994	+ 93		X
3/18/88	55.9%		2087	− 131		X
5/27/88		35.2%	1956	+ 228		X
10/21/88	51.5%		2184	− 92		X
12/2/88		27.6%	2092			

Dow points gained on advisors' predictions: +137
Dow points lost on advisors' predictions: −6,095
Net points gained on advisors' predictions: −5,958

Looking at Figure 25, you can see that on April 23, 1965, an extreme in optimism was hit as 89.7 percent of the advisory services were optimistic about the market. At the time, the DOW was at 911. By the time of the next advisory extreme, the market had dropped to 863. The advisory services were unjustified in their optimism! On July 30, 1965, the advisory sentiment hit another extreme; only 41.4 percent of the advisory services were positive about the market, indicating an extreme in pessimism. But by the next market extreme, the DOW had jumped 125 points; the advisory services were wrong again. Based on the data from Investor's Intelligence, the tracked advisory services were right only three times in indicating the direction of the market, those being February 21, 1975, March 1, 1985, and April 4, 1986.

Overall, Figure 25 shows results similar to Figure 24. Extremes in sentiment, whether optimistic or pessimistic, indicate an imminent change in the market. When market pessimism hits bottom, it's typically a good time to buy since the market will most likely be headed up. And when market optimism reaches a peak, it's often time to sell before the fall.

While you usually can't wait until market extremes develop before you buy or sell shares, you may be able to use the extremes to your benefit at some time. An extreme in market optimism may occur as you are selling shares. Or an extreme in pessimism may develop as you are buying. Extremes in consumer and market sentiment are just another historical tendency you may want to keep in mind.

CALENDAR-RELATED MARKET TENDENCIES

It's not always practical to wait until the market hits an extreme before you buy or sell fund shares. But there are other market tendencies you may be able to use to your advantage. Statistically, it has been shown that there are better times of the year, months of the year and days of the week to buy or sell fund shares. Like the market tendencies already mentioned, these are not trends you should necessarily seek out. They are, however, trends you may want to consider when you are planning to buy or sell.

Times Of The Year

The stock market closes for seven major holidays during the year – Easter (Good Friday), Memorial Day, July 4, Labor Day, Thanksgiving, Christmas and New Year's Day. Historically, since 1952, it has been found that market activity and prices preceding holidays have had an exceptional tendency to rise, especially on the last trading day prior to the holiday.

Figure 26, based on Martin Zweig's analysis of the market from January 1952 to June 1985, shows the direction of the market surrounding holiday periods. As you can see, most of the time the market was up.

Figure 26

Direction of the Market
Surrounding Holidays
1952-1985

Pre-holiday	Up	Down	Unchanged
Easter	26	5	3
Memorial Day	25	4	5
July 4	28	5	0
Labor Day	31	2	0
Thanksgiving	27	4	2
Christmas	25	7	1
New Year's	31	1	1

Post-holiday			
Thanksgiving	30	2	1
Christmas	22	10	1

The market was up 26 times before Easter, 25 times before Memorial Day, 28 times before July 4, 31 times before Labor Day, 27 times before Thanksgiving, 25 times before Christmas and 31 times before New Year's Day. Over the same time period, the market rose 30 times after Thanksgiving and 22 times after Christmas. Over a total of 299 holiday trading days, the market rose a total of 245 times, it declined 40 times and it was unchanged on 14 occasions. Thus, the odds are strong that the market will rise surrounding each of these holidays.

Why does the market tend to move up right before holidays? Probably because people are generally in a positive mood around holidays and are more likely to buy than sell anything, including shares of stock. This buying activity creates an upward trend in stock prices. The market has also shown very strong tendencies to move up on the day after Thanksgiving and Christmas, possibly because of continued holiday spirit. The day after Thanksgiving many employees are off from work. And it may be that the post-Christmas market optimism is due to people in good cheer between Christmas and New Year's.

What do these holiday tendencies mean for investors? If you're going to buy fund shares, anyway, it may be in your best interest to buy them several days before a holiday in order to increase your odds of getting off to a good start. On the other hand, if you're selling shares, you may want to wait until just before the market closes prior to the holiday, or even hold onto your shares to sell them on the first day the market is open after the holiday.

It may also be a good idea to watch the general trend of the market prior to the holidays. If the market does not move up, you should consider it a negative sign. This increases the probability that the market will go against the trend and fall or remain flat, instead of rising.

Obviously there are a limited number of holidays.

It may not be particularly feasible to wait until a holiday before you buy or sell shares. If, however, a holiday is approaching and you are planning on buying or selling shares anyway, you may want to consider the tendencies of the market surrounding holiday periods.

Year-End Tax Selling

Investors who hold depressed stocks frequently sell them late in the year to take advantage of the tax loss. They want to use their losses to offset taxable gains for the year. That's why the market has often been artificially depressed in the early part of December.

But many investors who sell stocks for tax losses intend to repurchase their shares 31 days later, in January. (If the shares are repurchased within 31 days, the tax benefit is lost.) Once investors have repurchased shares, the market has tended to rise. This phenomenon has been referred to as the "January effect."

Yet studies are showing that by the end of December, stocks which had been performing poorly are tending to improve somewhat. Part of this improvement is due to the market's upswing during the holiday season. It is also due to wary investors recognizing the market's tendency to rise in January. Anticipating the January effect, these investors are buying low-priced shares late in December. This buying activity has created a market upturn in mid-to-late December that is carrying over into January.

If you combine the market's mid-to-late December

upturn with the market's tendency to be up around the holidays anyway, the latter part of December can be a good time to sell shares. November through the middle of December may be a good time to buy shares as investors tend to sell, depressing the market. Remember, taking advantage of market extremes means doing the opposite of what the crowd is doing. Certainly you wouldn't want to wait until November to buy shares and December to sell shares. But if you are going to be buying or selling shares towards the end of the year, it might not be a bad idea to give this trend some consideration.

Months Of The Year

Just as the market tends to be up surrounding holidays, it tends to be up during certain months of the year, as several studies have shown. Figure 27, monthly DOW movement, is based on a study by Arthur A. Merrill of Merrill Analysis, Inc. It shows the percent of the time the DOW has risen during each month of the year from 1897 to 1988.

Figure 27

Monthly DOW Movement 1897-1988

Month	Percent of the time the DOW rose
January	64.1%
February	47.8%
March	58.7%
April	54.3%
May	48.9%
June	52.2%
July	59.8%
August	65.2%
September	41.3%
October	55.4%
November	59.8%
December	70.7%
Average for all months	**56.5%**

The market was found to be at higher levels during winter and summer. The DOW was up 70.7 percent of the time in December and 64.1 percent of the time in January, rises that may be partly attributable to the holiday season. July and August are the summer months in which the DOW has been at higher levels; the DOW was up 59.8 percent of the time in July and 65.2 percent of the time in August. September on the other hand, was the month in which the DOW was least likely to rise, followed by February and May.

Figure 28, monthly tendencies of the S&P 500 from 1926 to 1982, shows findings similar to Figure 27. Based on a study by Anthony Tabell, it was found that December and January were the months in which the S&P 500 was most likely to move up, followed by August, November and July. September was once again the month of the year in which the S&P 500 was least likely to rise.

Figure 28

Monthly Tendencies of the S&P 500 Index 1926-1982

Month	Upward Movement	Downward Movement
January	41	22
February	34	29
March	35	28
April	35	28
May	32	31
June	34	29
July	37	26
August	40	23
September	24	39
October	33	30
November	38	25
December	46	17

Another study by Merrill found that the market tends to be stronger than normal at the end of the month and the effect is likely to carry over into the beginning of the subsequent month. This tendency was found to occur for roughly the last three days of one month and the first six days of the following month. Studies by other analysts have shown similar patterns.

Based on these studies, to best make use of the market's monthly tendencies, you may want to buy shares during the months when the DOW or S&P 500 are least likely to rise, and sell during the months when they are most likely to rise. According to these statistics, September would be the best month in which to buy since that's when the market tends to be down, followed by May, June and February. Of course December would be the best month in which to sell, since it's at the end of December especially that the market tends to be up, followed by January, August, July and November.

It would not necessarily be to your benefit to wait to sell until the months when the market tends to be highest. And it may not make sense to buy only during those months when the market is lowest. However, if you are going to be buying or selling shares and a key buying or selling month is approaching, you may want to think about how you can make the best use of it.

Days Of The Week

Just like the tendency for the market to be up during certain months of the year, there is a statistical tendency for the market to be higher on certain days of the week. Is it any surprise that the market tends to be down on Mondays and up on Fridays?

Figure 29

Percent of Time the DOW Was Up
For Days of the Week 1952-1974

Monday	41.6%
Tuesday	51.8%
Wednesday	55.5%
Thursday	53.5%
Friday	59.8%
Average	**52.5%**

Figure 29 shows the percent of time the DOW was up for days of the week from 1952 to 1974. This study, also by Arthur A. Merrill, found that on average the DOW was up 52.5 percent of the time for all days of the week. On Mondays the market has tended to trail, being up only 41.6 percent of the time. By Wednesday, the market has tended to rise above average, although not significantly. Then a very slight market dip on Thursdays has been followed by a peak on Fridays, when the DOW has been up 59.8 percent of the time. Other studies looking at the movement of the S&P 500 found similar results for 1953 to 1970; Fridays the market tended to be highest and it tended to lag on Mondays.

What's behind these market tendencies? They are tied to consumer sentiment once again. Think about how most people feel on Mondays. By Friday people are in a better mood as they look forward to the weekend. What does this sentiment mean for investors? Based on the daily tendencies, if you are selling shares, you may want to wait until Friday; if you are going to buy, it may be best to buy on Monday.

Should you always wait until a specific day of the week before you buy or sell shares? Of course not. But if you are buying shares and the end of the week is near, you may want to consider waiting until the beginning of the following week before you buy. If you are selling shares and it is already Wednesday, you may want to think about waiting until Friday, if it is feasible. And even if you do follow these tendencies, there is no guarantee that the market will be higher on

Friday or lower on Monday. Just because the market has tended to follow such a pattern does not mean it will do so during the week you plan to move your money in or out of the market.

No Perfect Time to Buy or Sell

All of us would like to buy into a fund when the price per share is lowest and sell shares when the price is highest. Unfortunately, unless you can accurately predict the market, there is no way to be certain when that time occurs. If you wait for the perfect time, you may be losing out on investment opportunities. Such losses, as we have seen, are an even greater risk to take.

Timing the market is one buying and selling strategy that has resulted in a poor record of success. The odds of timing the market correctly, as statistics show, are not in your favor. But even if timing did work in theory, it is not a very practical approach to investing. Market timers need to constantly watch leading economic indicators and be prepared to make their moves. How many of us can afford the time and energy needed to analyze all of those data and track every market movement?

Dollar cost averaging is one of the easiest ways for anyone to buy or sell shares efficiently. By gradually moving your money into the market, you overcome the problems of investing when the market is at its peak, or liquidating when the market hits bottom. Your purchases and sales, over time, average out to a more favorable price per share.

Although there may not be a perfect time to invest, historical data have shown that there may be some better times to invest, if you are able to take advantage of them. According to historical statistics, extremes in market and consumer sentiment, holiday periods, certain months of the year and days of the week may present opportunities for you to buy shares at lower prices and sell them at higher prices. Often it's not practical to wait until a holiday, a particular month or day of the week to move your money into the market. But if you're planning to purchase stock or bond funds to meet your investment objective, these historical market tendencies may be of some assistance. You may wish to consider these tendencies when you are averaging into or out of the market.

If, for example, market and consumer sentiment are extremely negative and you had been planning to buy shares, you might be able to purchase them at a lower price. If you're selling shares as a holiday is approaching, you could possibly use the tendency for the market to be up surrounding holidays to your advantage. If you need to buy shares and you are aware that the market tends to be up on Friday, if it is feasible, you can wait until Monday or Tuesday, when the market has a greater tendency to be down.

These historical tendencies are not a means for predicting the up-and-down movements of the market, nor should these strategies be used to buy or sell frequently, as market timers attempt to do. These statistics merely indicate what has historically occurred in the market. Following these strategies does not guarantee that you will buy shares at the lowest prices possible or sell them at the highest prices. But considering what has tended to happen in the market when you are going to be buying or selling shares may increase your chances of buying and selling at more favorable prices.

Conclusion

To invest successfully, you need to select mutual funds that will provide you with the highest risk-adjusted returns. But if you are to meet your investment objectives, it is even more important that your portfolio be structured properly. Diversified Mutual Fund Investing provides you with a logical framework that is not only necessary but indispensable if you are to structure your portfolio. Yet it will also assist you in selecting mutual funds that produce the highest returns possible, within your risk parameters.

Building your Diversified Mutual Fund portfolio involves three basic steps. First, you must determine your investment objective. You need to decide whether you should structure your portfolio to provide you with growth, income, or some combination of growth and income. Here is the beginning of your own, personalized investment strategy.

Next, you must allocate your assets. You need to split your investment dollars between the growth, income and liquid asset categories. This step is essential if your returns are to help you meet your investment objective. Part of your allocation will also involve considering your risk tolerance; funds within various groups will produce different levels of returns at different levels of risk.

The third step in Diversified Mutual Fund Investing is fund selection. You can follow a specific methodology at this point to simplify your fund selection and help you maintain your portfolio. Although there are many mutual funds available, you need to concentrate only on the types of funds matching your investment objective. Then, after you thoroughly evaluate funds based on their risk as well as their return, you can pick the risk-adjusted performers that will best meet your investment needs.

While investing in mutual funds can reduce your risk, Diversified Mutual Fund Investing allows you to reduce your risk even further. You can, for one, easily combine fund selections from different asset categories within your portfolio. Although funds have different rates of returns and different types of risk, your overall returns should be more stable through a portfolio of funds.

By investing in mutual funds, you gain the skills and experience of some of the best money managers in the business. Fund managers are in a better position to select securities than individuals who are not involved in the financial marketplace on a full-time basis. They can objectively analyze all of the necessary data and make the most appropriate decisions regarding portfolio holdings. Diversified Mutual fund Investing provides you with yet another advantage in this regard. Through Diversified Mutual Fund Investing you can not only diversify among securities and asset categories, but among fund managers. By holding a portfolio of funds you will have not one but a number of fund managers working for you.

Is there risk in mutual funds? Of course there is. There is no such thing as a risk-free investment. But mutual funds reduce the risks of investing in individual securities without reducing your profits. By following Diversified Mutual Fund Investing, you can not only invest safely, but profitably. You can overcome the greatest obstacles found when dealing with individual securities or with mutual funds and thereby reduce your risk further. A properly structured portfolio holding mutual funds carefully selected to meet your investment objective can provide you with the highest returns at the lowest level of risk.

INDEX

return rating, 31
selection, 44
turnover, 73, 74
fund advisory services, 139
funds, number to select, 27

G

general corporate bond funds, 53, 100
general government bond funds, 54, 100
general municipal bond funds, 56
global bond funds, 55
global stock funds, 49
gold/precious metal funds, 50
government money market funds, 83
government mortgage-backed bond funds, 54
Government National Mortgage Association, (GNMA), 54
government treasury bond funds, 55
Gross National Product, 62
growth and income funds, 48, 89
growth and income objective, 97, 98
Growth Fund of America, 129
growth funds, 46
aggressive growth/ maximum capital appreciation, 47, 100
equity income, 48, 100
global stock, 49
growth & income, 48

international stock, 49, 95
large company, 47, 95
option income, 49, 100
small company, 47, 95, 100
specialty/sector, 50, 95, 97, 102
growth portfolio, 96

H

health funds, 51
high-quality corporate bond funds, 53, 89, 100, 102, 104
high-yield corporate bond funds, 53, 89, 102
high-yield municipal bond funds, 56, 89, 97
historical investment returns, 12-14
historical market tendencies, 131
calendar-related market tendencies, 143-155
extremes in market sentiment, 132
fund advisory services, 139-142
fund cash-to-asset ratios, 135
holiday-related market activity, 144
hybrid funds, 57, 117
asset allocation, 59
convertible bond, 59